ADVANCE PRAISE

Kevin Niu believes, as do I, in the power of sports to bring disparate people together. Through a series of impactful examples of international diplomacy, Kevin chronicles how sports have long served as a constructive force in creating commonality and empathy. His book reinforces why sports are one of the few remaining institutions that transcend borders, cultures, and languages and unite people around the world.

—**Adam Silver**, Commissioner of the National Basketball Association (NBA)

Pivotal moments have shaped global history. The story of Ping-Pong Diplomacy is one such moment—a seemingly small event that opened doors to dialogue and cooperation between two great nations. Yifei Kevin Niu's book captures the essence of how sports can transcend politics and bridge divides, bringing to life the nuanced and courageous diplomacy that my grandfather championed. It is a testament to the power of human connection, and a reminder that even in the most challenging times, a simple game can change the course of history.

—**Christopher Nixon Cox**, grandson of President Richard Nixon; Board Member, The Richard Nixon Foundation

A superb examination of the often overlooked role of sports in international relations by an impressive emerging leader and scholar. Yifei Kevin Niu is a gifted athlete, academic, and writer—as well as a passionate student of the role of sports in easing tensions between countries. As leaders, diplomats, and citizens around the world strive to employ all means of achieving common objectives, they would do well to consult Sports Diplomacy and be reminded of the critical role that sports can play in the pursuit of peace, understanding, and human connections in our increasingly complex world.

—**General David Petraeus**, US Army (Ret.), former Commander of the Surge in Iraq, US Central Command, and Coalition Forces in Afghanistan; former Director of the CIA; and co-author of the *New York Times* bestseller *Conflict: The Evolution of Warfare from 1945 to Ukraine*

Sports are easily forgotten these days as anything more than head-to-head combat for leisure entertainment. Yifei Kevin Niu, as a seventeen-year-old young American, reminds us all of what sportsmanship really means in this highly educational book. In a geopolitically fractured world today, we all should remember from the history that Kevin's book narrates that even the fiercest competition in the Olympic Games could bring about the best of humanity towards cooperation, unity, peace, and harmony, however adversarial circumstances had become. It is a very worthy read for any citizens of the world who are concerned but hopeful about our future.

—**María José Alcalá Izguerra**, four-time Olympian; president of the Mexican Olympic Committee

THE
DIPLOMATIC ARENA

UNTOLD STORIES IN INTERNATIONAL SPORTS

The Diplomatic Arena is published under Erudition, a sectionalized division under Di Angelo Publications, Inc.

Erudition

Erudition is an imprint of Di Angelo Publications.
Copyright 2024.
All rights reserved.
Printed in the United States of America.

Di Angelo Publications
Los Angeles, California

Library of Congress
The Diplomatic Arena
ISBN: 978-1-962603-25-6
Paperback

Words: Yifei Kevin Niu
Cover Design: Savina Mayeur
Interior Design: Kimberly James
Editors: Matt Samet, Willy Rowberry

Downloadable via www.dapbooks.shop and other e-book retailers.

For educational, business, and bulk orders, contact distribution@diangelopublications.com.

1. Sports & Recreation --- History
2. Sports & Recreation --- Cultural & Social Aspects
3. Political Science --- International Relations --- Diplomacy

THE

DIPLOMATIC ARENA

UNTOLD STORIES IN INTERNATIONAL SPORTS

YIFEI KEVIN NIU

Acknowledgments

I owe this work to a long list of mentors, friends, and family members—all of whom deserve credit and recognition for their contributions.

First and foremost, I would like to thank all my mentors. My English teacher and varsity-tennis coach Leon Calleja, who has been, and continues to be, incredibly supportive of my pursuit of sports writing and my sports newspaper, *The GOAT*. Richard Lui, who took me under his wing and guided me into real-life journalism. Jing Qian and Yi Qin, as well as everyone else at Asia Society, who have inspired me to connect with youth from all over the world through a common interest in international relations. Mike Schoenleber and the Nixon Family policy proposal members, for welcoming me into their team of incredible collaborators and offering me an opportunity to contribute to such an important report. Lastly, Professor Niall Ferguson, who not only provided academic guidance but also best exemplified the highest scholarly excellence.

Thanks to my friends at Andover, who have been honest with me: Daniel, Bodhi, Avery, Charles, Anthony, and Zach, to name just a few. My high school life would not have been as meaningful and memorable without all of you. To Will, Isaac, Marcello, Ben, Jeremy, Chris, Jesse, and Luka, who always make me feel like I never left home.

Forever and always, a special thanks to my family. My

laolao and *laoye,* who spent many years taking care of me. My *nainai* and *yeye,* who beam with pride every time they see me. My sister, who is always there for me, even if she doesn't let me know. My dad, for setting a great example of striving for the highest ambition. And my mom, who is the magic that glues our family together, and whose unconditional love provides the coziest harbor for me to come home to.

Contents

Introduction

Sport has the power to change the world. It has the power to inspire. It has the power to unite people in a way that little else does. It speaks to youth in a language they understand. Sport can create hope where once there was only despair. It is more powerful than governments in breaking down racial barriers.

—Nelson Mandela, South Africa's first
democratically elected President[1]

Beyond the thrill of competition and the roar of the crowd, the world of sports plays a vital role in international relations, serving as a tool for public diplomacy, building connections, promoting national identity, and influencing political decisions on the world stage.

One of the most visible ways nations engage in sports diplomacy is by hosting major sporting events. The Olympics and the FIFA World Cup, in particular, draw global attention and provide a platform for nations to showcase their cultural heritage, organizational capabilities, and hospitality. The successful execution of such events can enhance a country's image on the world stage and create lasting positive perceptions. For example, the 2008 Summer Olympics in Beijing, widely considered "a coming-out party" for China, showcased the country's economic prowess and cultural richness, altering international perceptions and paving the way for increased diplomatic engagement. Similarly, the 2014 Winter Olympics in Sochi, Russia, allowed the nation to present itself as a capable and modern host despite the geopolitical tensions surrounding the event.

Achieving success in elite sports provides an alternative avenue for states to elevate their global standing. Athletes become cultural ambassadors, embodying the values and prowess of their nations on the international stage. A prime example is East Germany, where athletic achievements in the 1970s served as a powerful tool for gaining global recognition as a separate state from West Germany. These athletes, dubbed "diplomats in tracksuits," represented national excellence and helped establish East Germany's distinct identity on the global stage.[2] Similarly, Cuba has also utilized the success of its boxing and baseball stars to project a positive national image on the international scene.[3] In 1984, China signaled its strength as an emerging world power with a fourth-place ranking in gold-medal counts at its first-ever Summer Olympics,[4] along with its astounding rate of economic growth in the 1980s.

While these types of sports diplomacy are most common, this book goes beyond competition to explore the lesser-recognized but more potent ability of sports to promote cultural understanding and exchange between peoples, thereby revealing sports as a unique tool for establishing and improving diplomatic relations on a more personal level. As we will see, cultural exchange forms the bedrock for building stronger diplomatic ties between nations. When individuals from different cultures develop a sense of understanding and respect for each other, it becomes easier for their governments to collaborate and find common ground on various issues. This bottom-up approach to diplomacy, in which cultural understanding precedes political negotiations, can prove more resilient and sustainable than agreements solely based on political expediency.

The power of sports diplomacy is best exemplified by the transformative role of Ping-Pong Diplomacy in thawing the historically tense relations between the United States and China in the early 1970s. Triggered by an unexpected invitation for a U.S. table tennis team to visit China in 1971, the tour, in its diplomatic significance, extended far beyond the sport itself. Ping-Pong Diplomacy served as a classic icebreaker, providing a neutral ground for behind-the-scenes talks that ultimately paved the way for President Richard Nixon's historic visit to China in 1972. This unconventional form of diplomacy, rooted in sports, was pivotal in reshaping the geopolitical landscape, helping normalize diplomatic relations between the two nations. Another example is how baseball games between the United States and Japan played a crucial role in the aftermath of World War II in promoting goodwill and rebuilding diplomatic ties. In the 1990s, baseball emerged again as a significant catalyst in thawing the long-standing diplomatic tensions between the United States and Cuba. The agreement that allowed Cuban athletes to play in Major League Baseball without defecting contributed to a gradual warming of relations between the two nations during a period marked by diplomatic challenges.[5]

Whereas traditional public diplomacy struggles for audience and impact, sports diplomacy holds immense potential. "I think there are two common languages globally, ... one of them is sports, and the other one is music," said Sarah Hirshland, CEO of the U.S. Olympic and Paralympic Committee.[6] As a medium for international communication, reputation-building, and relationship-building, sports have unparalleled influence and global reach. The substantial financial investments made worldwide in sports surpass government expenditures on traditional public diplomacy efforts. Sports not only command colossal global audiences but also generate a level of interest that eclipses other subjects, including political news and movies. Meanwhile, the notion of sports, notably the Olympic Movement, as a force for world peace has been challenged to suggest that other applications of sports in international affairs may be more impactful, including examples from the Cold War era where nations strategically used sports competitions as a demonstration of their political virtues and a nonviolent way to assert dominance over adversaries.[7]

This book describes landmark moments in sports diplomacy. Each chapter begins with a historical overview of the conflicts that made the sporting event significant, followed by a detailed account of the event. For key events, I have also included interviews with individuals who have intimate knowledge of the occurrences.

Chapter One

The Little Ball That Moved the Big Ball

I had never expected that the China initiative would come to fruition in the form of a ping-pong team.

—Richard Nixon, 37th president of the United States[8]

Among the many examples of sports diplomacy, none is more consequential than Ping-Pong Diplomacy. A series of exchanges between the American and Chinese national table tennis teams led to President Richard Nixon's historic visit to China in 1972, known as "the week that changed the world."[9]

THE CHANCE ENCOUNTER

The year was 1971. Once allies in World War II, China and the United States had not had diplomatic relations for more than twenty years. In fact, no American had officially been allowed to set foot in China since 1949.[10]

Nineteen-year-old American table tennis player Glenn Cowan was excited to attend Nagoya, Japan, for the 31st World Table Tennis Championships. On one fateful March afternoon in the big Japanese city, he missed his bus but soon got on another one heading to Aichi Stadium. As the bus started to move, he felt dozens of eyes staring at his back. On the back of his uniform were three large letters: U.S.A. On the bus were twenty-five Chinese players and delegation members.

At a time when the United States was considered "the No. 1 enemy" in China because of its capitalist views and opposition in the Korean and Vietnam wars, table tennis took on a political mission. According to the Chinese leader Chairman Mao Zedong, "Regard a ping-pong ball as the head of your capitalist enemy. Hit it with your socialist bat, and you have won the point for the fatherland."[11]

On the bus, because the Chinese players were not allowed to make contact with Americans, they all froze at the presence of this interloper. Cowan, unshaken thanks to his untraditional personality, broke the silence by asking if anyone spoke English. Seeing an interpreter nodding, Cowan loosened up, saying, "I know my hat and hairstyle and clothes look funny to you, but in the U.S. lots of people look like this."[12]

At this moment, Zhuang Zedong, a three-time world singles champion, stood up from the last row and made his way forward. He told Cowan through the interpreter that the Chinese and American people have always been friendly with each other, and that he was very happy that Cowan had come that day. He then gave Cowan a handmade silk tapestry of China's famous Yellow Mountain.[13] Cowan was totally star-struck. Everybody knew Zhuang Zedong! Cowan fumbled through his gym bag for a gift in return but came up empty-handed.

The ride was short, but history was made. At the stadium, the group met with journalists, who captured photos of a blue-eyed American among a bus full of Chinese people. Caught on film, the exchange between Cowan and Zhuang was a moment of unexpected goodwill between the American and Chinese teams. Chairman Mao later commented that Zhuang Zedong was a good table tennis player and diplomat.[14]

Fueled by the Japanese media, news of Zhuang's friendly exchange with Cowan spread like wildfire. The next day, Cowan gave Zhuang in return a T-shirt with a peace symbol and the lyric/song title "Let It Be" by the Beatles. When asked by a journalist if he wanted to visit China, Cowan replied, "Of course!"—a seemingly impossible wish and request at the time. The Chinese government had already planned to invite table tennis players from several countries, including the United Kingdom, Australia, Colombia, Canada, and Nigeria, to visit China after the Championships. However, the United States was not under consideration. Would the Americans be allowed to go to China? After all, like its Communist ally Russia, China had been closed off to the United States for over twenty years due to its differing political ideology. All eyes were on Beijing.

The viral conversation and formal request from the American team caused quite a stir in Beijing. After some deliberation, China's Ministry of Foreign Affairs and the State Sports Commission decided that the time was not yet right. They reasoned that the United States had not shown sincerity on the "Taiwan issue"—China's contention that the liberation of Taiwan was an internal issue in which no other country could interfere—and was still invading Vietnam, Laos, and Cambodia, threatening China's security. It was also unusual to receive a U.S. sports team in China prior to hosting any American diplomats. Although Premier Zhou Enlai had been working tirelessly on ways to restore communication with the United States, he eventually sided with the Ministry of Foreign Affairs, and reluctantly sent the decision to Chairman Mao Zedong for review. The subject of rapprochement between the two countries had been weighing heavily on Mao's mind of late. Earlier that evening, Premier Zhou talked to him about the progress made through the Pakistani and Romanian channels, and the U.S. State Department's announcement on March 15, 1971, to lift all restrictions on travel to China for U.S. passport holders.

As fate would have it, Chairman Mao had a change of heart after taking some sleeping pills, according to Jung Chang and Jon Halliday, in their book *Mao: The Unknown Story*.[15] Consequently, the U.S. table tennis team was invited to visit China as it was preparing to leave Nagoya. In Nagoya, the deputy head of the U.S. table tennis delegation, Rufford Harrison, was drinking coffee when he learned of China's official invitation. He stood up and threw the coffee like champagne into the air—everyone knew he had not been holding out much hope for a positive response! He later recounted, "I was in this case a Daoist, even though Dr. Kissinger [at the time the National Security Advisor] considered me a 'daring young man on the flying trapeze.'"[16]

In Beijing, it was Premier Zhou Enlai who had issued the

official invitation to the American team to visit China. Given the visit's diplomatic significance, Zhou ordered relevant personnel to quickly draw up a detailed plan for receiving the American guests. In Washington, DC, President Nixon promptly approved the U.S. team's visit. In 1967, when he'd been Eisenhower's vice president, Nixon announced that he no longer supported a policy of isolating China. In 1970, fearing that any goodwill toward China's Communist Party would be harshly criticized, President Nixon had Kissinger reach out to Premier Zhou through highly secretive back channels.[17] On the last day of the World Table Tennis Championships, Nixon was pleasantly surprised by a major diplomatic development.

The U.S. team accepted the invitation and crossed into China from Hong Kong on April 10, 1971.[18]

THE VISIT

The visit was historic in every sense. The U.S. delegation, consisting of nine table tennis players, four officials, two spouses, and three journalists, was the first non-communist group of Americans to set foot in China since 1949.[19] *Time* featured a photo of the Americans in front of the Great Wall in the article "The Ping Heard Round the World."[20] On April 15, a huge banner displaying "Hello China!" appeared in the British newspaper *The Daily Mirror*, announcing China's opening to the world.[21]

Precious photographs and passport images from Connie Sweeris, one of the players who traveled to China, gave us a rare glimpse of the historic trip. The photo taken on the tarmac at the airport in Beijing shows the first American delegation to stand next to Chinese officials in a quarter of a century.[22]

When the U.S. team accepted the invitation, U.S. Department of State consular officials in Japan made a seemingly trivial but monumental change to their passports. The word "China" was carefully crossed out by hand on the page stating, "This passport is not valid for travel to or in communist-controlled portions of...,"[23] signifying the beginning of history-making events far more significant than table tennis matches.

As a strategic move, Chinese Premier Zhou Enlai granted visas to foreign journalists to ensure global coverage.[24] During their weeklong stay in China, the U.S. team played exhibition matches, later immortalized by the Oscar-winning film *Forrest Gump*. The Americans got to experience China firsthand, finding themselves in an utterly foreign country that had been closed off to the world for decades. From the People's Republic of China's founding in 1949 up until President Richard Nixon visited in 1972, the country maintained a "Bamboo Curtain," mirroring the Soviet Union's "Iron Curtain" in closing off China to the outside world. In China, people wore plain clothes, rode bicycles, and listened to government-approved music. In the United States, people wore vibrant colors, drove private cars, and listened to disco. Yet deep down, the curiosity to get to know the other culture and the desire to connect at a human level were the same between the two peoples. The players once again exchanged gifts, with every moment captured by international journalists.

A member of the U.S. table tennis delegation marveled, "People are just like us. They are real, they're genuine, they got feelings. I made friends, I made genuine friends, you see. The country is similar to America, but still very different. It's beautiful. They got the Great Wall, they got plains over there. They got an ancient palace, the parks, there's streams, and they got ghosts that haunt; there's all kinds of, you know, animals. The country changes from the south to the north. The people, they have a, a unity. They really believe in their Maoism."[25]

At the end of their trip, the delegation met with Zhou Enlai, who talked about "a new chapter in the relations of the American and Chinese people," as embodied by the photo of Premier Zhou shaking hands with the American player Connie Sweeris. Zhou and Cowan, the American player who'd started the chain of events, exchanged ideas about the American hippie movement.[26]

Halfway around the world, President Nixon announced that the United States was easing trade restrictions against China. Three months later, the two governments opened back-channel communications, resulting in a secret trip to Beijing by Kissinger. Ten months after the meeting between the Chinese Premier and the U.S. table tennis delegation, President Nixon became the first U.S. president to visit China after decades of diplomatic stalemate. In April 1972, one year after the U.S. team had visited China, the Chinese table tennis team reciprocated the visit by coming to the United States to play at Stanford University and the University of Michigan.[27]

BEYOND U.S.-CHINA DIPLOMACY

Ping pong, formally known as table tennis, was and still is not popular in the United States. At the time of the

World Championships in Nagoya, the U.S. men's team was ranked 24th in the world and had to borrow funds to attend.[28] However, table tennis helped two major international adversaries bridge the Cold War gap, a feat that had not been accomplished by other means at the time. China, however, has long used sports as a diplomatic tool, built on the idea of "friendship first, competition second."[29]

Ping-Pong Diplomacy came onto the world stage once more in 1991, when a unified Korean team from North and South Korea played together at the World Table Tennis Championships in China. They again fielded a joint team in the 2018 World Team Table Tennis Championships in Sweden.[30]

With Armenia and Turkey at bitter odds in 2008, Turkey's president, Abdullah Gul, attended a World Cup qualifier soccer match after accepting a historic invitation from his Armenian counterpart, Serge Sarkisian. It was the first time that senior level officials of the two countries had met. The president of Armenia later referenced Ping-Pong Diplomacy in *The Wall Street Journal:* "Just as the people of China and the United States shared enthusiasm for ping-pong … the people of Armenia and Turkey are united in their love of football."[31]

Before the International Table Tennis Federation changed the official ball size to 40 millimeters in 2000, ping-pong balls measured a mere 38 millimeters (1.5 inches) in diameter, three-trillionths of the diameter of the earth. Yet, as covered in the next two chapters, table tennis promoted dialogue, stronger diplomatic ties, and cultural exchange around the globe. When "the little ball moved the big ball,"[32] history witnessed "the week that changed the world."[33]

Chapter Two

The Week That Changed the World

Forty years ago, even those of us who are alive and conscious of what was going on in the world still have a hard time computing the kind of seismic change that has occurred.

—Tom Brokaw, anchor of *NBC Nightly News* and White House correspondent[34]

THE TIMING

With his signature wit and humor, Tom Brokaw, in speaking of China's Bamboo Curtain, explained, "China might as well had been one of those medieval maps that said, 'Beyond here, serpents lie.' It was a completely closed society. We had no relationship with it whatsoever. You did not dial 1-800-Zhou-Enlai. Mao Zedong did not have a Facebook. There was no dotcom China or Beijing. And it took [America] two years to establish real contact with the Chinese."[35]

The U.S. table tennis delegation's visit to China could not have come at a more opportune time. President Nixon and Chairman Mao had been looking for an opportunity to reconnect the nations. China, after years of the Cultural Revolution and decades of isolation, was eager to open up to the world. President Nixon had been interested in engaging China since he'd taken office in 1969, with the goal of containing a potential nuclear power and weakening the Sino-Soviet relationship.[36] As Nixon's handwritten notes revealed, "Chinese Communists: Short range – no change. Long range – we do not want 800,000,000 living in angry isolation. We want contact. China – cooperative member of international community and member of Pacific community."[37]

THE ACTION

In his report to President Nixon on July 14, 1971, Kissinger, having met with Premier Zhou on July 9 during his "secret trip," described Zhou as someone who "ranks with Charles De Gaulle as the most impressive foreign statesman I have met." Kissinger concluded, "We have laid the groundwork for you and Mao to turn a page in history. But we should have no illusions about the future ... the process we have now started will send enormous shock waves around the world."[38]

On July 15, 1971, President Nixon asked for airtime on national TV to announce that Premier Zhou, on behalf of the Chinese government, had invited him to visit China, and that he'd accepted this invitation "with pleasure,"[39] sending a shock to the world. *The Washington Post* commented, "If Mr. Nixon had revealed he was going to the moon, he would not have flabbergasted his world audience more."[40]

On February 21, 1972, Nixon met with Mao Zedong and Zhou Enlai to discuss the first "Joint Communiqué" in Shanghai.[41] During the visit, both countries pledged to work toward "normalization" of relations and to expand "people-to-people contacts" and trade opportunities. It was the beginning of a series of rapidly developing events that laid the groundwork for the formal re-establishment of U.S.-China relations. On April 12, the Chinese table tennis team visited the United States on a two-week tour, as described in the previous chapter, and was received by President Nixon in the White House. On June 19, Kissinger worked "to promote normalization" on his second visit to China. On June 23, U.S. House of Representatives majority and minority leaders arrived in China for a two-week visit. On February 22, 1973, after Kissinger's third visit to Beijing, the United States and China agreed to establish "liaison offices" in each other's capitals. On July 4 of that year, Chase Manhattan Bank and the Bank of China established a corresponding relationship, making it the first time a U.S. bank had worked with a Chinese bank since 1949. On July 8, 1973, the U.S. Postal Service announced parcel-post delivery between the United States and China. On October 25, 1974, George H.W. Bush, the new head of the Liaison Office, arrived in China and met with Chinese Vice Premier Deng Xiaoping. On January 1, 1979, the United States and China established full diplomatic relations. U.S.-China relations have continued to this day, developing into the world's most economically important bilateral relationship.[42]

THE SIGNIFICANCE

President Nixon's visit to China led to what he called "the week that changed the world." Its far-reaching significance cannot be overstated.

Ping-Pong Diplomacy was the stimulus needed to break the ice age that had lasted twenty-two years between China and the United States, from 1949 to 1971. The formal diplomatic relations established subsequently under President Carter promoted interactions in science, academia, business, and tourism between the two countries. Many sister cities and states/provinces were established, creating extensive ties between the two societies.

Nixon's visit was also a brilliant strategic move for U.S. national security, fundamentally changing the balance of power within the "strategic triangle" (the United States, China, and the Soviet Union), forging an alliance between the United States and China against the Soviet Union. This power shift, in turn, put Moscow under increasing geopolitical pressure and weakened the Soviet Union. Eventually, the collapse of the Berlin Wall (1989) and the disintegration of the socialist regimes in Eastern Europe ushered in the end of the Cold War.[43]

Lastly, as a result of the United States' engagement with China, other governments that had previously isolated and contained China followed suit in normalizing relations. Within a year of Ping-Pong Diplomacy, China successively established or restored diplomatic relations with thirty-eight countries, including Australia, Mexico, Spain, Germany, Japan, and the United Kingdom.[44] In this sense, Nixon's visit not only thawed U.S.-China relations; it also opened up China to the world, contributing to China's economic growth and rise to global power.

Ending China's isolation is one of the motivations for Nixon's groundbreaking visit to China. In the fifty years since Ping-Pong Diplomacy, China has systematically integrated into the international order, essentially achieving Nixon's global strategic goal of 1967: "Taking the long view, we simply cannot afford to leave China forever outside the family of nations... There is no place on this small planet for a billion of its potentially most able people to live in angry isolation."[45]

While many historical events have changed the world, it is undeniable that President Nixon's China visit remains of lasting importance, having made enormous contributions to China's opening up and the ensuing decades of peace between the two world powers after two bitter proxy wars in Korea and Vietnam. Today, fifty years later, the two countries are at a crossroads again, with increasingly hostile attitudes. Nevertheless, deep down, there is an inherent affection between the two peoples. The pendulum could swing in a more positive direction, perhaps with another push from sports diplomacy.

CHAPTER THREE

THE RIPPLE EFFECT THAT TRANSCENDED SPORTS

Ping-Pong Diplomacy was a huge success for one key reason—it humanized all of us to the other side. We wanted to introduce the Chinese to a number of segments of American life and society, to show them that we as Americans were human. It also had the benefit of showing the Americans that the Chinese were human as well. It then enabled us ... to build a series of exchanges that gradually over the years brought more and more Americans and Chinese into contact with one another and made us realize that, at heart, we are all human beings.

—Jan Berris, Vice President of the National Committee on U.S.-China Relations[46]

Fifty-plus years ago, the humble ping-pong ball served as a prelude to re-establishing U.S.-China relations; today, the people's diplomacy that changed the international order is still reverberating in its historical impact. The most profound lesson of Ping-Pong Diplomacy is that breakthroughs in global affairs rely on friendship and bilateral trust built between two peoples. Ping-Pong Diplomacy knocked down the first domino and created momentum for rapid cultural exchange between the United States and China.

SCIENTIFIC EXCHANGES

In February 1971, the National Academy of Sciences in the United States contacted the president of the Chinese Academy of Sciences through the Royal Swedish Academy of Sciences to express a desire to establish contact with Chinese scientists.[47] However, the Chinese side did not respond due to the nonexistent diplomatic relations between China and the United States. This situation changed abruptly at the start of Ping-Pong Diplomacy.

In April 1971, while conducting research in North Vietnam, Arthur Galston, a botanist from Yale University, and Ethan Signer, a biologist from MIT, learned of the U.S. table tennis team's unexpected invitation to visit China. They made a request to the Chinese Embassy in Paris to visit China, which was later approved by the Ministry of Foreign Affairs on behalf of Chairman Mao and Premier Zhou. An invitation was sent out by the China National Tourism Administration and the China Association for Science and Technology. In early May 1971, Drs. Galston and Signer arrived in China from Vietnam, becoming the first American scientists to visit since the founding of the People's Republic. They visited research institutions and universities, held discussions with Chinese scientists, and met with Zhou Enlai in Shanghai.[48]

After returning to the United States, Drs. Galston and Signer advocated for the benefits of increasing exchanges with Chinese scientists. Their visit to China led to the reciprocal visits of delegations from the American Association for the Advancement of Science and the Chinese Academy of Sciences in 1972, further reopening the door for academic and technological exchange.

A Chinese Medical Association delegation visited the United States from October 13 to 31, 1972, at the invitation of the National Institutes of Health and the American Medical Association. This historic visit marked the first time a medical and scientific delegation from the People's Republic of China had been to the United States.[49] The unprecedented collaboration allowed scientists to see "the opportunity for, first, diplomacy for science and, then, science for diplomacy."[50] Scientific interactions had significant political implications and contributed to the normalization of U.S.-China relations under President Carter, built on the previous efforts of Nixon, Kissinger, and Gerald Ford.

CULTURAL EXCHANGES

In October 1971, during Henry Kissinger's second visit to China, he officially proposed to Zhou Enlai that the two countries engage in exchanges in science and technology, culture, sports, and news. After the news announcement that U.S. President Nixon would visit China in 1972, there was a surge in applications from all sectors of the United States to visit and engage in exchanges with China. Visits of various sports and cultural delegations snowballed, including gymnastics, basketball, volleyball, and football teams, the

Chinese Acrobatic Troupe, the Chinese Martial Arts Team, and the American Symphony Orchestra. In the fall of 1972, a delegation from the American Society of Newspaper Editors visited China, a trip that was reciprocated by twenty-one Chinese journalists coming to the United States in May 1973. In December 1972, the Shenyang Acrobatic Troupe toured four American cities. In September 1973, the Philadelphia Orchestra made a historic visit to China, performing Western classical music and overwhelming a Chinese audience of 8,800.[51]

In April 1972, the same trip mentioned in chapter 1, the Chinese table tennis team came to the United States, playing a sold-out exhibition game at Cole Field House at the University of Maryland. Robert Hormats, the former Under Secretary of State who served as a senior economic adviser to three White House National Security Advisers from 1969 to 1977, wrote in *The Hill,* "The Chinese team's tour was a huge success, not just because the matches were fun to watch, but also—and more importantly—because the Chinese delegation met with everyday Americans." This up-close-and-personal contact helped to mitigate many of the negative feelings toward China prevalent among Americans at the time. "They personalized the relationship for everyday Chinese and Americans in ways that would have been hard to do through other channels," commented Hormats.[52]

In a short period after Ping-Pong Diplomacy, the United States and China established 50 sister provinces and states and 232 sister cities, reflecting the importance of this people-to-people exchange, one that was critical in breaking down old, negative stereotypes, such as the view of the Chinese as the "red peril" or the "yellow hoard."[53] From May 1971 to early February 1972, over 100 American scientists, doctors, scholars, and journalists were received in Shanghai. Following Nixon's visit to China, from mid-1972 to mid-1973, almost a thousand Americans visited Shanghai, a fivefold increase from the previous year.[54]

PEOPLE-TO-PEOPLE DIPLOMACY

In July 1978, Frank Press, Science Advisor and Director to President Carter, led the first scientific delegation to China. This was the highest-level scientific delegation at the time to visit a foreign country in U.S. history. Chinese leader Deng Xiaoping suggested to Press that the United States should accept 700 Chinese students; his larger goal was for the United States to accept tens of thousands of students in the coming years. Press was surprised by this suggestion and immediately called Carter in Washington to ask for his approval, which Carter granted. Within the following five years, approximately 19,000 Chinese students came to the United States to study. There are now close to 300,000 Chinese students enrolled in American schools.[55] Press also helped form the National Committee on Scholarly Communication with the People's Republic of China.[56]

Premier Zhou Enlai once pointed out that China's diplomacy combines official, semi-official, and people-to-people diplomacy.[57] After diplomatic relations between China and the United States were normalized, they still went through various ups and downs, but people-to-people diplomacy has never faltered and has played an irreplaceable and unique role, especially when official and semi-official relations encounter difficulties.

A befitting anecdote to end this chapter may be one shared by Robert Hormats. When he met the visionary Chinese leader Deng Xiaoping years after Ping-Pong Diplomacy, Hormats mentioned playing table tennis with the world champion Zhuang Zedong. When Deng joked about knowing who had won, Hormats said Zhuang had generously let him win a few points out of kindness. Deng replied, "A gesture of respect for you and America. That should remind you that we Chinese do believe in cooperative outcomes. Each side should gain something. Of course, if we do win a few points from time to time, you should not hold this against us. We have a lot of very talented people."[58]

INTERVIEW WITH JIM BYRON

James T. (Jim) Byron is president and CEO of The Richard Nixon Foundation, and a member of the foundation's board of directors. He is overseeing the American Civics Campaign, a $40 million effort launched in 2023 to reacquaint middle school and high school students with American civics and history.

Yifei Kevin Niu: *What does Ping-Pong Diplomacy represent for The Nixon Foundation?*

Jim Byron: Ping-Pong Diplomacy was a diplomatic masterstroke that began as an event of sheer happenstance. At an international tournament in Japan in 1971, an American player mistakenly boarded a bus full of Chinese players. A subsequent invitation for the American team to visit China—and become the first American delegation to visit China in nearly twenty-five years—gave Chairman Mao an opportunity domestically to persuade the Chinese people that a rapprochement with the United States was in China's national interest. President Nixon had already been making diplomatic moves to signal to the Chinese government that his administration would welcome a dialogue, which he first outlined in a 1967 article in *Foreign Affairs* magazine and began to put into practice very early in his administration. After years of secret and delicate negotiations between the two governments, the result was the February 1972 visit of President and Mrs. Nixon to China for perhaps the most important state visit of the second half of the twentieth century.

YKN: *How does The Nixon Foundation commemorate or educate the public about the events surrounding Ping-Pong Diplomacy?*

JB: The Nixon Foundation designed and funded the museum galleries at the Nixon Library, which opened in 2016 after a $25 million renovation. The largest exhibit on the Nixon presidency is about President Nixon's trip to China. Ping-Pong Diplomacy and its legacy are commemorated with four paddles that were given to President and Mrs. Nixon, now on display for the public to see and appreciate.

Today, The Nixon Foundation interacts regularly with members of the Chinese-American community and welcomes tourists from China to learn more about the interaction of Chinese and American history and culture in the twentieth century, thanks to President Nixon's historic and groundbreaking trip in 1972.

YKN: *How has the legacy of Ping-Pong Diplomacy influenced subsequent efforts to use sports as a means of promoting international relations by The Nixon Foundation?*

JB: In 2008 and again in 2011, The Nixon Foundation welcomed the original Ping-Pong Diplomacy players from 1971—on both the Chinese and American sides—for gameplay exhibitions in the Nixon Library's beautiful East Room ballroom. Representatives from the U.S. and Chinese Olympic Committees attended the "rematch games," and *Sports Illustrated* covered the events.

YKN: *From your perspective, what lessons can be learned from the success of Ping-Pong Diplomacy in bridging political divides, and how might these lessons be applied to current geopolitical challenges?*

JB: It was a matter of sheer happenstance that the Chinese and American players came across one another and interacted as they did in 1971; this strengthens the point that international sporting competitions can bridge divides between disparate or different peoples and cultures. The 2028 Olympics in Los Angeles will be another opportunity for The Nixon Foundation to engage in the often-overlooked intersection between sports, history, and culture.

YKN: *Are there ongoing initiatives or partnerships between The Nixon Foundation and other organizations to promote the role of sports in fostering international understanding and cooperation?*

JB: President Nixon was a sports enthusiast who regularly followed baseball and football. He rooted for both the California Angels and the New York Mets (despite being a good friend of Yankees owner George Steinbrenner) and once called Super Bowl play while on the phone mid-game with Redskins coach George Allen. In recent years, The Nixon Foundation hosted an exhibit at the Nixon Library on the history of baseball, and counts the Los Angeles Angels of Anaheim as an institutional partner.

CHAPTER FOUR

THE OLYMPIC MOVEMENT THAT CELEBRATED HUMANITY

Wars break out because nations misunderstand each other. We shall not have peace until the prejudices that now separate the different races are outlived. To attain this end, what better means is there than to bring the youth of all countries periodically together for amicable trials of muscular strength and agility?

—Pierre de Coubertin, founder of the modern Olympics and the International Olympic Committee (IOC)[59]

THE OLYMPIC MOVEMENT

Founded on the principles of peace, athleticism, and international collaboration, the Olympics serve a more profound purpose than just crowning the fastest and the strongest. They promote dialogue, understanding, and even peace. Inspired by the ancient Greek tradition of an Olympic Truce—the idea that the gods would safeguard the athletes and their loved ones throughout the event—the modern

Games, as envisioned by Pierre de Coubertin, encourage peaceful competition as a substitute for war.[60] Born into the French aristocracy, de Coubertin became a visionary of the common people, setting out to include sport in French education. After failing to convince French schools of the importance of physical education, however, Coubertin began to work toward the revival of the ancient Olympic Games. In 1894, after founding the IOC, Coubertin presented his idea during a conference in Paris, France, at which 79 delegates from 9 countries unanimously approved it. Coubertin pitched that "the most important thing in the Olympic Games is not to win but to take part, just as the most important thing in life is not the triumph but the struggle." The idea was so popular that the first modern Olympics was held just two years later, in 1896, hosting 280 participants from 13 nations competing in 43 events. While this ideal of peaceful rivalry in lieu of war hasn't always been a reality, the Olympics still provide a platform for nations to engage in friendly competition through a sense of shared humanity.[61]

The Olympic Movement aims "to contribute to building a peaceful and better world by educating youth through sport practiced in accordance with Olympism and its values."[62] Central to the Olympic Movement are its core values of excellence, friendship, and respect. Through the pursuit of athletic excellence, athletes from diverse backgrounds showcase determination and the universal human capacity for achievement. One notable example of the Olympics having helped political tensions is the 2000 Sydney Olympics, during which North and South Korean athletes marched together under a unified flag, signaling a moment of detente between the two nations.[63] Furthermore, the Olympic Movement actively promotes social and environmental responsibility. Initiatives like the Olympic Refugee Team (a group made up of independent Olympic participants who are refugees) exemplify the movement's commitment to inclusivity and the power of sports to overcome geopolitical challenges.[64]

The Olympic Movement achieves its goals in several ways. Athletes from different countries living and training together can break down cultural stereotypes. Sharing meals, competing side-by-side, and experiencing the thrill of victory and agony of defeat together build understanding and respect, creating goodwill between nations that might otherwise be locked in political disputes. Additionally, the Games can be a catalyst for social change. For example, the 2008 Beijing Olympics put a spotlight on China's environmental practices, leading to some significant improvements, such as the reduction of the industrial use of coal in and around Beijing in order to improve air quality.[65] The 2014 Sochi Olympics focused international attention on Russia's draconian LGBT laws.[66] While not a complete solution, the Olympics can force countries to confront issues that might otherwise stay hidden.

Of course, the Olympic Movement has faced criticism. Accusations of corruption, doping scandals, and the immense cost of hosting the Games have tarnished its image. Additionally, using the Olympics as a platform for political messages, as witnessed during the Cold War when the United States and the Soviet Union boycotted each other's Olympic Games (1984 Los Angeles and 1980 Moscow), highlights the potential for abuse. Despite these challenges, the Olympic spirit of peaceful competition remains a powerful force.

THE OLYMPIC FLAG

The Olympic flag is an integral part of the Olympic tradition. First introduced during the 1920 Antwerp Games, the Olympic flag has since become a universally recognized symbol of the Olympic Movement. The flag features five interlocking rings, each of a different color—blue, yellow, black, green, or red—intended to represent the unity and diversity of Earth's many nations.[67] These colors were chosen because at least one of them appears on the flag of every nation in the world. Meanwhile, the rings interlock to signify "the union of the five continents and the meeting of athletes from throughout the world at the Olympic Games," representing the coming together of the world's nations in the spirit of friendly competition and international cooperation.[68]

The designer of the Olympic flag was Pierre de Coubertin; as described higher, he was inspired by the ancient Greek Olympics, which also used a symbol to represent the unity of the participants. In ancient Greece, it was a flame carried from Olympia to the Games' host city. Today, this ancient tradition is still carried out with the Olympic-torch relay. The Olympic flag is raised at the Games' opening ceremony and lowered at the closing ceremony. It is also flown at the Olympic Village and all Olympic-related events. The Olympic flag is a powerful symbol of the Olympic spirit and the values of the Olympic Movement: excellence, friendship, respect, and fair play.

In addition to the Olympic flag, the Paralympic flag was introduced during the 1960 Paralympic Games and featured three "agitos," or three arrows in red, blue, and green. These three colors represent the three colors most widely found in national flags. The agitos are arranged in a triangle to symbolize motion and bringing people together: "always moving forward and never giving up."[69]

OLYMPIC TRUCE

Dating back to ancient Greece, the Olympic Truce—as mentioned before—was founded on the idea that the gods would safeguard the athletes and their loved ones throughout the event. A temporary pause in hostilities between city-states was believed to facilitate secure passage to and from the Games, allowing athletes and spectators from all regions to attend. The concept of the truce was also rooted in the Greek mythological figure Ekecheiria, the personified spirit of truce and armistice. Widely admired during the Games, a statue of Ekecheiria was in the Temple of Zeus at Olympia.[70]

Any violation of the Olympic Truce resulted in a prohibition from participating in the Games and a fine for the transgression. One such instance occurred during the Olympic Games in 420 BC when the Spartans were believed to have attacked a fortress and sent hoplites to invade Elis. Despite the allegations, the Spartans refused to pay the fine, resulting in a twenty-year ban from entering the holy site of Olympia and participating in the Games.[71]

The ancient Olympic Games were organized to end conflicts and foster harmonious relationships. When the modern version of the Games was inaugurated in 1896, it carried on the legacy of its predecessor by maintaining a commitment to global peace and the advancement of humanity. In modern times, the United Nations General Assembly reaffirms the

Olympic Truce before each edition of the Olympic Games. The truce encourages the use of sports to promote peace and diplomacy and has been endorsed by all 193 member states of the United Nations.

CHRISTMAS FOOTBALL TRUCE

The Christmas Truce of 1914 was a remarkable moment in modern history—a brief but powerful episode of peace and humanity during the horrors of World War I. This spontaneous ceasefire, particularly highlighted by the impromptu football matches played between opposing forces, allowed for an escape from the brutality of the war.

The Christmas Truce occurred in the first year of World War I (1914–1918). By December 1914, the Western Front had become a grim stalemate, with soldiers entrenched in muddy, freezing conditions. Despite the pervasive violence, there were underlying sentiments of shared suffering and a yearning for peace among the troops. In early December, Pope Benedict XV called for a temporary cessation of hostilities during the Christmas period, but the warring governments officially rejected this appeal. However, the soldiers on the front lines, motivated by their own desires for a reprieve from the relentless fighting, took matters into their own hands. On Christmas Eve and Christmas Day of 1914, soldiers from both sides of the conflict initiated informal truces along various stretches of the Western Front. The most documented instances occurred between British and German troops in sectors of Belgium. The ceasefire began with soldiers singing carols and exchanging greetings across No Man's Land. Eventually, some soldiers bravely ventured out of their trenches to meet their adversaries.[72]

One of the most enduring images of the Christmas Truce is that of the informal football matches played between opposing forces. Accounts of these matches, though varied in detail, consistently describe soldiers using makeshift balls or tin cans as balls. The impromptu matches were a momentary return to normalcy and human connection, starkly contrasting the surrounding desolation and death. Sadly, this fleeting moment of peace did not alter the course of the war. Fighting resumed shortly afterward, and similar large-scale truces did not reoccur in subsequent years. However, the truce left an indelible mark on the collective memory of World War I. Football matches, in particular, have come to represent the enduring human spirit and the possibility of reconciliation even during conflicts. The truce underscored the profound disconnect between the political agendas driving the war and the soldiers' experiences in the trenches.[73]

UNITING EAST AND WEST, NORTH AND SOUTH

An irrefutable example of the power of sports to transcend politics is the joint team of East and West Germany at the 1956, 1960, and 1964 Olympic Games, as well as the unified team of North and South Korea at the 2018 Olympic Winter Games. These teams were formed despite irreconcilable political differences, even if only for a brief moment.

East and West Germany

The aftermath of World War II left Germany a shattered nation, physically and politically, one divided into four occupation zones. No surprise then that a desire to compete in the Olympics emerged in the newly formed Federal Republic of Germany (West Germany) and the German Democratic Republic (East Germany). Despite the countries' shared history, the ideological divide between communism and democracy created a rift between the two Germanies, one that soon extended to sports. Both nations sought recognition on the international stage, yet their rivalry and mutual distrust complicated their Olympic aspirations.

The path to Olympic participation was filled with political maneuvering and diplomatic negotiations. The specter of the Cold War made the idea of a unified German team a political minefield. While West Germany established its own National Olympic Committee and gained recognition from the IOC in 1951, East Germany's attempts to do the same were met with resistance. The IOC initially rejected East Germany's bid for a separate Olympic Committee, leading to strained relations between the two German states.[74] Despite these tensions, a pragmatic solution emerged in 1955: a unified German team for the 1956 Olympics. While the introduction of a new flag by East Germany sparked controversy, the question of anthems was easily resolved with the adoption of Beethoven's "Ode to Joy."

On the field, the 1956 Games proved relatively successful for the unified team, garnering a gold and a bronze in the Winter Games and six gold, thirteen silver, and seven bronze medals in the Summer Games. However, the façade of unity began to crumble in 1959, with the source of friction being the flag. East Germany's adoption of a flag incorporating communist symbols clashed with West Germany's vision of a unified national symbol. The proposed compromise by the IOC—a modified flag with Olympic rings—failed to appease West Germany's government, which threatened a complete withdrawal from the 1960 Games.[75] The issue of visas for East German athletes competing in the 1960 Winter Games in the United States further strained the relationship.[76]

With the construction of the Berlin Wall in 1961, mutual distrust escalated, leading to restrictions on athlete movement between the two Germanies and the end to the dream of a unified German Olympic team. The fall of the Berlin Wall in 1989 marked a turning point, paving the way for German reunification politically and on the Olympic stage. After forty-five years of competition as separate teams, a single German Olympic squad returned in 1990, symbolizing the nation's long-awaited unity.[77]

North and South Korea

A defining moment of the 2018 Olympic Winter Games in Pyeongchang, South Korea, was the last-minute decision to unite the host nation's women's hockey team with their North Korean counterparts, a baby step on the path to peace and reconciliation on the divided Korean peninsula. As detailed in the book *A Team of Their Own: How an International Sisterhood Made Olympic History*, the story of the joint team reveals cultural clashes between North and South Korean players as well as unexpected friendships forged on the ice.[78]

While their underdog status translated into a last-place finish, the unified Korean team went far beyond wins and losses in terms of its impact. The formation of the team itself was a dramatic tale. While discussions about Korean unification on the ice had been simmering since 2001, it was only finalized three weeks before the Olympics. Korean-team head coach Sarah Murray, who was initially skeptical, acknowledged the unique experience of having players from opposing ideologies share a locker room. Despite some initial apprehension, Murray soon discovered that there were "smiling girls" beneath the political uniforms, not the robotic figures she had envisioned.[79]

The prospect of North and South Korean athletes competing together resonated deeply with the global audience. As the team took to the ice, it radiated a sense of hope that eclipsed longstanding animosities and geopolitical tensions. During the opening game against Switzerland, the true story unfolded on the sidelines. Kim Yo-jong, the sister of the North Korean leader Kim Jong-un, sat alongside South Korean president Moon Jae-in, witnessing the symbolic power of sports in the presence of the IOC president Thomas Bach.[80]

As the world reflects on the legacy of the joint hockey team, questions remain about the future of inter-Korean sports collaboration. South Korea and North Korea have explored further unification efforts for sports like judo and basketball. While it may be premature to say the 2018 Korean women's hockey team will jumpstart Korean reunification, its legacy lies in offering a glimpse of possibility—a testament to the unifying spirit of sports and the potential for peace on the Korean peninsula.

OLYMPIC BOYCOTTS

Throughout the past 100-plus years, the Olympic Games have served as a stage for the world to come together in the spirit of athletic competition and international cooperation. However, behind the pageantry and athletic prowess lies a complex web of political intrigue, in which the ideals of sport intersect with the realities of global diplomacy. One of the most controversial manifestations of this intersection is the phenomenon of Olympic boycotts, wherein countries abstain from participation in the Games as a form of protest or a political statement.

The practice of boycotting the Olympic Games dates back to the early twentieth century, but it was during the Cold War era that boycotts became a prominent feature of Olympic politics. The first major boycott occurred in 1956, when several nations, including the Netherlands, Spain, and Switzerland, withdrew from the Melbourne Olympics in protest of the Soviet Union's invasion of Hungary. That same Games, Egypt, Iraq, and Lebanon withdrew in response to the Suez Crisis when Israel invaded Egypt. This marked the beginning of a trend wherein the Olympic Games became a battleground for ideological conflicts between the East and West.[81]

However, the 1980 Summer Olympics in Moscow ushered in a new era of Olympic boycotts, with the United States leading a coalition of countries in boycotting the Games to protest the Soviet Union's invasion of Afghanistan. Over sixty nations, including traditional Olympic powers such as Canada, West Germany, and Japan, joined the boycott, dealing a significant blow to the legitimacy and integrity of the Games. Their decision was deeply divisive, with proponents arguing that it was a necessary response to Soviet aggression. At the same time, opponents criticized the boycott as a politicization of sport that punished athletes for the actions of their governments. The boycott had far-reaching consequences, not only for the athletes who were denied the opportunity to compete but also for the Olympic Movement as a whole, which was left reeling from the fallout.[82]

In retaliation, the Soviet Union and its allies boycotted the 1984 Summer Olympic Games in Los Angeles, further exacerbating the tensions between the East and West. The absence of key nations from the LA Games cast a shadow over the competition and raised questions about the future of the Olympic Movement in an increasingly polarized world.[83]

Subsequent Olympic boycotts, such as those seen in the 1988 Seoul Olympics and the 2008 Beijing Olympics, have continued to underscore the fraught relationship between sport and politics. While some argue that boycotts are a legitimate means of expressing dissent and holding host countries accountable for their actions, others caution against the weaponization of sport for political ends, warning that such actions undermine the unity and universality of the Olympic Games. Olympic boycotts also raise several ethical concerns. The athletes who train their entire lives for the Games are often the ones who suffer the most—denying them the opportunity to compete on the biggest stage can be considered unfair. Additionally, boycotts can further isolate nations and hinder potential dialogue and diplomacy.

When questioned about the effectiveness of sports boycotts, "It's the athlete that fundamentally suffers ... and I don't think anyone has ever been able to prove that a boycott makes any difference," said Retired Gen. Martin Dempsey, a former chairman of the Joint Chiefs of Staff, suggesting that there is little evidence to support the notion that the six boycotts in Olympic history accomplished their objectives.[84]

OLYMPIC TRAGEDIES

Since its inception, the Olympic Games have seen an increasing amount of conflict. By remembering and learning from the following events, we can continue to uphold and strengthen the values the Olympics represent. By acknowledging the past, we can work toward a future where the Games embody their true ideals of peace, unity, and athletic excellence.

The year 1912 marked the start of the fifth Olympic Games in Stockholm, which were held while Europe was on the brink of WWI. Coubertin, inspired by the sacred truce of the ancient Olympics, proposed that the sixth Olympic Games be held in Berlin in order to alleviate the impending disaster. The Hungarian Olympic Committee supported Coubertin's proposal by withdrawing Budapest's request to host that event. Although the German government agreed to hold the Games in Berlin, the outbreak of World War I in 1914 shattered Coubertin's dream of the "sacred truce." The Berlin Olympics became the first in modern Olympic history to be canceled.[85] Subsequently, the Tokyo Olympics in 1940 and the London Olympics in 1944 were also canceled due to World War II.

In addition to the impact of world wars I and II, the

Olympics have also been affected by acts of terrorism and political conflict.[86] On September 5, during the 1972 Munich Olympics, members of the Palestinian militant group Black September infiltrated the Olympic Village, killing 2 and taking hostage 9 Israeli athletes and coaches. The situation quickly escalated, and the terrorists demanded the release of over 200 Palestinian prisoners held in Israeli jails. The German authorities attempted a rescue mission, but it ended in disaster, resulting in the deaths of all remaining hostages and a German police officer. The world watched in horror as the tragedy unfolded, with many expressing their outrage and disbelief at the senseless violence. The attack profoundly impacted the Munich Games, with many questioning whether it was appropriate to continue the event. Despite calls for cancellation, the IOC decided to continue the Games, stating that it would be a tribute to the victims. The remaining events were marked by a somber atmosphere, with the Olympic flag flown at half-mast and a memorial service held to honor the fallen.

In the aftermath, many countries hosting future Games implemented new security measures to prevent similar incidents. The IOC heavily pressured organizers of subsequent Games to spend more on security, with the 1976 Montreal Games spending over 50 times more than Munich had. (In 2008, China spent $6.5 billion on security alone.) The IOC also soon provided a fund to support the families of the Munich victims. The Munich massacre contributed to a safer environment not just for the Olympics but for all sporting events. It sparked a global discussion on the relationship between politics and sports, in which many people, including athletes, officials, and fans, argued that political conflicts and tensions should be kept separate from sporting events.[87]

Twenty years later, the 1992 Barcelona Olympics would not only be impacted by the war in Yugoslavia but also by sanctions imposed by the United Nations (UN). By mid-1991, Yugoslavia had been split into two different bodies, Serbia and Montenegro. Due to the region's ongoing conflict and humanitarian crises, it was placed under sanctions by the UN. These sanctions included arms embargoes, economic restrictions, and limitations on participation in international events, such as the Barcelona Games. These sanctions were part of broader efforts to restore peace and stability in the Balkan region and to hold accountable those responsible for war crimes. Because the war continued through 1992, the IOC was faced with a difficult decision regarding Yugoslavian athletes. In the Olympic spirit, the IOC reached an agreement with the UN to allow individual Yugoslav athletes to participate as Independent Olympic Participants under the Olympic flag. This decision upheld the Olympic spirit of peace and unity while addressing the grave geopolitical realities of the time.

That same year, the IOC temporarily recognized the National Olympic Committee of Bosnia and Herzegovina and invited them to participate in the 1992 Games. This decision was made in light of the ongoing conflict in Bosnia and Herzegovina and the need to promote peace and unity through sports. Based on a joint proposal by the IOC and the UN, the warring parties in Bosnia were able to cease hostilities during the Barcelona Olympics. In 1993, the IOC submitted the Olympic Truce proposal, jointly signed by 184 national Olympic committees, to the UN. With the support of Secretary-General Boutros Boutros-Ghali, the proposal was unanimously adopted by 121 countries attending the UN's forty-eighth session on October 25, 1993. The proposal requires all UN member states to abide by the Olympic Truce requirements beginning one week before and extending until one week after, respectively, the opening and closing ceremonies of the Olympics. Beginning in 1994, the president of the United Nations General Assembly traditionally initiates a Solemn Appeal for the observance of the truce during the Olympics, which extended to the Paralympic Games starting in 2006. For example, ahead of the 2024 Paris Games, UN Secretary-General António Guterres delivered a heartfelt message: "In the spirit of the Olympic Truce, I call on everyone to lay down their arms, build bridges, foster solidarity, and strive for the ultimate goal: peace for all."[88] Remembering the tragedies in Olympic history reminds us of the impact of political and social issues on global events—these tragedies have also tested and ultimately reaffirmed the core values of the Olympic Movement. The determination to continue the Games is a commitment to Olympic ideals and the belief in the power of sports to unite people.

INTERVIEW WITH KIM VANDENBERG

Kim Vandenberg is an American swimmer and Olympic bronze medalist (2008 Beijing Olympics). Vandenberg also won a silver medal at the 2007 World Swimming Championships and gold at the 2011 Pan American Games. She is an ambassador for Room to Read, an organization that focuses on literacy and gender equality in education.

Yifei Kevin Niu: *Can you describe any moments when you were brought together with other cultures because of swimming?*

Kim Vandenberg: As an Olympic swimmer and former professional athlete, I had the pleasure of traveling the world to compete, teach, lecture, and volunteer for sports-related programs. At numerous competitions abroad, including the Olympic Games, people from all around the world came together to race. Swimming our best was the ultimate goal; even though we didn't speak the same languages, we understood one another, as we shared the same passion. I was also lucky to have been able to train in Europe after competing in the Olympics, specifically in Italy and France, where I swam with an international group of professional and Olympic swimmers. I was able to study new languages, taste new cuisines, and learn about different cultures.

YKN: *What role do you believe the Olympics play in fostering international relationships, beyond just competition?*

KV: There are three core values of the Olympic movement: excellence, respect, and friendship. With these three themes, the world comes together and shares the dream of becoming the best it can be. Respect and friendship are concepts that foster positive relationships beyond any competition. The Olympics inspire people to be their best selves, and this inspiration breeds an understanding of our shared human experience. With understanding comes unity. It's a team effort to become your best. You have coaches, teammates, support staff, family, and friends who encourage you to be at your best. This team mentality brings people together. Even if there is conflict on the team, hopefully it will be discussed and explored in a healthy environment. These relationships built within teams will ideally transfer over outside of sports, in relationships with coworkers and family members, etc.

YKN: *What makes sports such a universal language?*

KV: Sports and music are two activities that unite the world instead of divide us. Swimming opened many doors to travel and, with that, gave opportunities to respect other people's differences while also exploring new ways of seeing the world. Sportsmanship requires respect, determination, and admiration of your competitors; through my pursuit of being a good sportswoman, I had the chance to meet and become friends with people from around the globe. It was an absolute honor to be able to travel as extensively as I did and to swim at the Olympics in 2008.

CHAPTER FIVE

THE SPORT THAT SAVED
U.S.-JAPAN RELATIONS

*This [baseball] trip is the greatest piece of diplomacy ever. All the
diplomats put together would not have been able to do this. …
[Lefty O'Doul had done] more to establish friendly relations with
[Japan] than 100 diplomats.*

—General Douglas MacArthur, Supreme Commander for the
Allied Powers (1945–1951)[89]

*Words cannot describe Lefty's wonderful contributions, through
baseball, to the postwar rebuilding effort.*

—General Matthew Ridgway, Supreme Commander for the
Allied Powers (1951–1952)[90]

INTERNMENT OF JAPANESE AMERICANS

Baseball is known as America's national pastime, and there is no other ethnic group that has embraced the sport as much as Japanese Americans. Horace E. Wilson, an American educator, baseball enthusiast, and Civil War veteran, was credited with bringing baseball to Japan. In 1871, Wilson arrived in Japan with a baseball and bat in his suitcase. As he embarked on a three-year contract to teach at the newly established Kaisei Academy in Tokyo, baseball quickly became a captivating diversion for his Japanese students during their free time. The game gained popularity among players and spectators alike, and by 1876, the Japanese team was ready to compete against an American team made up of American teachers and ex-pats in Tokyo.[91] Japan quickly embraced baseball as a means of shaping its modern national identity, incorporating this sportive aspect of Western culture during the transformative Meiji era—a period during which the Japanese people moved beyond being an isolated feudal society by embracing Western technological influences. When Japanese immigrants came to America during the late 1800s, they carried a love for baseball, setting them apart from other immigrants who were unfamiliar with the sport.[92]

Japanese-American baseball flourished as Japanese immigrants assimilated into mainstream America in the 1920s and 1930s. Nearly every Japanese community had a baseball team, and segregated ethnic leagues thrived across Japanese settlements. Enthusiastic crowds gathered for matches, with attendance often reaching the thousands for major games. Beyond recreation, baseball helped shape the concepts of ethnic identity within a rapidly expanding

Japanese-American population, strengthening the closely connected community despite their marginalization within larger American society.

In December of 1941, all sports came to an abrupt halt for Japanese Americans. Japan's swift and unexpected attack on Pearl Harbor thrust the United States into World War II. The war, which had seemed distant and abstract as Americans watched it from afar, became a tangible reality overnight. The attack on Pearl Harbor solidified the perception of "Yellow Peril," which was reignited by West Coast nativists. Coined by European imperialists in the nineteenth century, Yellow Peril wrongly portrayed Asian people as an existential threat to Western civilization. The ensuing collective hysteria toward individuals with Japanese backgrounds catalyzed a shift in transforming the enemy from a soldier on a physical battlefield to, in an ideological sense, taking a dim view of all Japanese people. "I'm for catching every Japanese in America, Alaska, and Hawaii now and putting them in concentration camps," stated Congressman John Rankin of Mississippi in 1942. On February 19, 1942, President Roosevelt's administration interned all individuals of Japanese descent with Executive Order 9066, displacing around 122,000 people to remote incarceration camps while liquidating their possessions.[18]

The camps were designed to segregate and vilify their inhabitants. Yet, the baseball the internees played there emerged as an unexpected medium through which War Relocation Authority personnel were confronted with the humanity of the detainees. For many Americans, the wartime rhetoric of a monolithic enemy clashed with the reality of Japanese individuals with families, aspirations, and a love for baseball—this very American sport. By shifting internees from abstract threats to individuals with real feelings and genuine interests, baseball eroded the dehumanizing effects of incarceration on the internees. This humanization, in turn, made it considerably more challenging to sustain the image of Japanese Americans as hypothetical enemies. Kenichi Zenimura, later credited as a pioneer in Japanese-American baseball, was an internee at the Gila River internment camp south of Phoenix, Arizona, who dedicated himself to nurturing the Japanese-American baseball scene during the internment period.

For the more than 110,000 internees, while barbed-wire fences separated them from the outside world, prejudice and discrimination caged them within the very land of the free. Throughout World War II, baseball provided a sense of normalcy and resistance against the dehumanizing effects of internment. It also symbolized hope, allowing Japanese Americans to assert their dignity and showcase their humanity. Soon after internees arrived at the internment camps, they began working on designing and constructing baseball diamonds. Despite the barbed wire, watchtowers, and barracks, Zenimura and a group of volunteers took on the daunting task of clearing sagebrush and devising methods to control dust at the arid Gila River internment camp. "It was a great hardship for everyone being in the camp because nobody had anything," said Kiyoko, Zenimura's wife. "Building the ballpark really saved us. It kept the spirits of the people up and helped everyone to stay positive and not become angry and short tempered."[94] Zenimura understood that baseball would be a recreational distraction and a vital necessity, mustering the unwavering spirit of the Japanese-American community at its darkest hours.

Despite their imprisonment by the U.S. government, the Gila River internees were able to take immense pride in American baseball upon finishing the field. One internee, Takeo Suo, recalled, "Putting on a baseball uniform was like wearing the American flag."[95] Soon, the baseball field became a place where the community could connect: "The teenagers and the adults would gather every night to watch the games," described Pat Morita, another internee who later starred as Mr. Miyagi in The Karate Kid, to Sports Illustrated. "I [was] sitting and cheering with a couple of thousand rabid fans."[96] Gila River's newfound pastime spread to other camps, such as the Jerome Center in Arkansas, whose internees' dedication motivated War Relocation Authority officials to help by providing dynamite to remove tree stumps, reflecting their belief in the internees as productive members of society.[97]

As baseball continued to gain popularity with the Japanese-American population, 16 internment camps, known as assembly centers, were created along the West Coast. One of these camps, Merced Assembly Center, housed 4,453 Japanese internees and soon became home to the Livingston Dodgers and the Cortez Wildcats. The different assembly center teams competed in 13 contests for the "Assembly Center Honor."[98] By the 1944 baseball season, there were signs of eased restrictions for Nikkei inmates who were considered "loyal" to the United States.[99] An editorial in the Gila News Courier wrote that "suspicious people in the nearby communities eventually accepted internees as one of their own."[100] The War Relocation Authority, shifting away from wartime hysteria, allowed internees to reuse material from old watchtowers to improve the Gila River baseball field. As the internees dismantled a wooden watchtower, once a symbol of restriction within the camp's confines, the timbers now found a new purpose as seats and stands for baseball games. The War Relocation Authority officials even decided to provide buses for internees to journey between camps unguarded when they wore baseball uniforms, a gesture that conveyed a sense of greater acceptance of the Japanese as Americans.

At the end of the 1944 season, Zenimura organized a comprehensive, thirty-two-team interment-camp league classified into three divisions based on skill level: A, B, and BB. Like the major leagues, Zenimura's league had an all-star team and a most valuable player. This new league was exciting, and in hopes of increasing competition, many teams traveled long distances to play against other camps. These baseball games were far from ordinary: the athletes from Gila River, Arizona, Heart Mountain, Wyoming, and other camps who participated in this series were labeled "enemy aliens." Still, Zenimura's new league had successfully connected much of the interned Japanese-American community through baseball.

While the Pearl Harbor attack was devastating to Japanese assimilation in America, the internment camps did bring more attention to Japanese-American baseball. The Brooklyn Dodgers' owner, Branch Rickey, showed significant interest in Japanese-American baseball players. He expressed his support in an open letter to all incarceration centers, stating, "The fact that these boys are American boys is good enough for the Brooklyn Club."[101] As a part of an innovative plan, he invited Nisei players to participate in open team tryouts. Rickey's statement, made two years after Jackie Robinson's groundbreaking debut in Major League Baseball (MLB), resonated a nation struggling with its ideals of inclusivity and the persistent reality of racial discrimination. When stating that Japanese Americans were simply "American boys," Rickey had reframed the narrative by challenging the ingrained idea that ethnicity determined one's Americanness.

Looking back on why he decided to build a baseball field at Gila River, Kenichi Zenimura recalled a story from his childhood in which he'd witnessed baseball's ability to humanize. In Livingston, California, there used to be billboard-sized stating "No Japs Wanted." Then, someone somehow arranged a game between the local Fresno Japanese Baseball Club and a non-Japanese team from Livingston. The Japanese team gathered enough courage to make the trip and played a great match. As games increased between the two communities, the signs disappeared.[102] This memory was one of the many reasons Zenimura was so passionate about constructing a baseball field at Gila River in 1942.

The internment period came to an end in 1945. On June 27, 1952, the McCarran Walter Act was passed, permitting a small number of Japanese people to enter the United States as legal immigrants and allowing Issei, like Kenichi Zenimura, to become naturalized U.S. citizens.[103] As the anti-immigration laws were lifted for Asian Americans and more Sansei athletes began to show their talents, the uphill battle to get into the major leagues began. In 1950, Wally Yonamine of Okinawa became a notable athlete when he tried out for the San Francisco Seals under manager Frank "Lefty" O'Doul, who praised Yonamine's all-around skills, especially his throwing, fielding, and hitting. Players like Wally Yonamine broke racial and cultural barriers that would let future generations succeed in the major leagues.

In a 1959 *Sports Illustrated* article that showed the post-war aspirations of many Japanese-American players, Mark Harris eloquently wrote: "In the person of Fibber Hirayama,[104] whose ancestry is Japanese, whose techniques are American and who contains in fine balance within himself his double heritage, the humiliated but emerging city of Hiroshima glimpses the ideal fusion of West with East."[105] To this day, there is no evidence proving that Japanese Americans were a threat to America. Before President Ronald Reagan signed the Civil Liberties Act of 1988 acknowledging the fundamental injustice of the internment camps, President Gerald R. Ford recognized, "We now know what we should have known then—not only was the evacuation wrong, but Japanese Americans were and are loyal Americans."[106]. When President Joseph R. Biden proclaimed February 19, 2022, as a Day of Remembrance of Japanese American Incarceration During World War II, he said, "We also uplift the courage and resilience of brave Japanese Americans who, despite being unjustly incarcerated, formed powerful communities and marshaled incredible dignity and strength."[107] Throughout those dark days of the internment camps, baseball had embodied the best of the two cultures, offering a hopeful vision for a nation where diverse heritage and assimilation could coexist.

"[For America], the meaning and design of the country

is so evident in its games. In many odd ways, America is its sports," wrote Roger Rosenblatt, a journalist at *Time* magazine and PBS NewsHour.[108] In reflecting social dynamics, sports have always allowed marginalized communities to challenge stereotypes. However, baseball took on a different meaning for Japanese Americans during World War II. "Without baseball, camp life would have been miserable," said George Omachi, who was interned in Arkansas and later became an MLB scout.[109] More importantly, baseball allowed the internees to transform themselves from "enemy aliens" into relatable humans.

While the Japanese internment period was a time of stark departure from the nation's ideals and values, baseball provided conscientious Americans with opportunities to witness the inherent humanity of the internees and reflect on their own moral compasses. This, in turn, helped improve the detainees' quality of life. For example, the War Relocation Authority's decision to place the Zenimura family in an Arizona camp was a humane gesture to help Kiyoko's battle with tuberculosis, as War Relocation Authority officials believed the dry climate in Arizona could be beneficial for her health.[110] Mrs. George Reid of Chicago gathered young Children's Society of Christian Service members to organize a fundraising bazaar, selling cookies to purchase reading materials for the Gila River camp.[111] Many Americans, including Secretary of the Interior Harold LeClair Ickes, the baseball great Sam Rice, and the future poet laureate of America Carl Sandburg, all welcomed evacuees to work on their farms.[112]

The power of baseball was also witnessed by Bernie

Weinstein, an American player on the Tucson Badgers who played the Japanese at an internment camp. He recalled, "I saw the fence and said, 'God, this is like a prison.' It was a game that most of us will never forget. I realized that these people were Americans, just like myself. The more I thought about it, the more I thought, what a big mistake we made by putting these people in this relocation camp." The two teams bonded over watermelon and a modest picnic after the game. The players from Gila River even demonstrated the art of sumo wrestling to the Badgers. Baseball had created a heartfelt moment of genuine connection during a time when the United States was at war with Japan. "The two coaches, Kenichi Zenimura and Hank Slagle, were ahead of their time," remarked the baseball historian Bill Staples Jr. "They were trying to teach their ballplayers the concept of shared humanity."[113]

REBUILDING U.S.-JAPAN RELATIONS

In the aftermath of World War II, the United States and Japan found themselves still on opposite sides of a bitter conflict, with deep-seated animosities and distrust lingering long after Japan's surrender. Yet, among the rubble and ruins of war, a curious phenomenon emerged that would play a pivotal role in rebuilding relations: baseball.

By the time World War II erupted, baseball had become a popular sport in Japan, with its own professional league and devoted fan base. However, it was the arrival of American troops in Japan during the post-war occupation that truly transformed baseball into a vehicle for diplomacy and reconciliation. Recognizing the potential of baseball to bridge cultural divides and foster goodwill, General Douglas MacArthur, the Supreme Commander of the Allied Powers in Japan, encouraged the sport's revival as part of his efforts to democratize and rebuild Japanese society. Baseball stadiums, repurposed as military barracks during the war, were reopened to the public, and American soldiers organized exhibition games with local teams.[114]

One of the most iconic moments in the history of U.S.-Japan baseball diplomacy came in 1949 with the San Francisco Seals tour. In 1949, Lefty O'Doul led the San Francisco Seals on a groundbreaking baseball tour of Japan, during which he was determined to use baseball as a tool for reconciliation and understanding between the two nations. Through O'Doul's vision and the Seals' spirited performances in playing against various American and Japanese baseball teams, the tour became a remarkable display of cultural exchange and mutual respect, leaving a lasting impact on both nations.

Lefty O'Doul wasn't your average baseball player. His established rapport with Japan—boosted by previous visits and his influence among professional Japanese players, through his manual of drills and game strategy—made him the perfect ambassador. Upon his arrival with the San Francisco Seals at Shimbashi Station in Tokyo, a massive crowd estimated at nearly one million people greeted him throughout the streets, highlighting the Japanese people's desire to move forward from the war.[115] O'Doul's mission was clear from the outset: to use baseball as a tool to build friendship and understanding. Despite initial apprehensions, particularly among players who had fought in the Pacific during World War II, O'Doul remained resolute in his pursuit of positivity and sportsmanship. His determination prevailed even in the face of sporadic unsportsmanlike behavior from Japanese fans, such as their hurling soda bottles at the Seals players.[116]

The tour kicked off with a series of games against various American and Japanese teams, drawing large crowds and an enthusiastic reception. O'Doul's Seals showcased their talent and professionalism, earning respect from both their opponents and the Japanese public. One standout moment came during "Kids Day" in Osaka, during which thousands of children had the opportunity to watch the Seals play.[117] O'Doul's commitment to inclusivity and youth engagement underscored the tour's broader mission of nurturing future generations of diplomats and leaders through the universal language of baseball.

Despite facing formidable opponents, including the All-Japan All-Star team, the Seals maintained their competitive edge while displaying humility and respect for their hosts. Cliff Melton's stellar pitching and Reno Cheso's hitting played in a downpour exemplified the team's resilience, which resonated with the Japanese fans. This act of sportsmanship solidified the bond between the teams and the audience— O'Doul praised the Japanese fans' enthusiasm, even joking that it was "natural for Seals to win in water."[118] Off the field, O'Doul and his players engaged in various other cultural exchanges, including impromptu clinics for Japanese university ballplayers and interactions with sumo wrestlers.

The tour itself served as a testament to O'Doul's vision. The Seals faced a variety of Japanese teams in spirited contests, showcasing their skills while maintaining the highest respect for the game. Wins and losses mattered less than mutual admiration and a shared passion for baseball. Japanese players, like the retired pitcher Kyoichi Nitta, noted the Seals' strategy and sportsmanship, recognizing them as valuable lessons.[119] American reporters observed O'Doul constantly teaching his players, even during games.

The tour culminated before Emperor Hirohito, who honored O'Doul and his team for their efforts in promoting goodwill between the nations. Back in the United States, General MacArthur hailed the tour as a resounding success, recognizing O'Doul and the Seals for their role in advancing diplomatic relations through baseball. The tour had not only showcased the talent of American players but also highlighted the evolution of Japanese baseball and its potential for international recognition.[120]

Overall, the tour's impact was positive: The Seals exposed Japanese players to a higher level of competition, highlighting areas for improvement. Through his interactions and guidance, O'Doul inspired a generation of Japanese players, his emphasis on fundamentals, sportsmanship, and dedication laying the groundwork for the future growth of Japanese baseball. Legends like Tetsuharu Kawakami sought his advice, and O'Doul's critiques on Kawakami's stance proved his desire to see Japanese players improve.[121] And finally, at one game, the sight of American soldiers making room for Japanese orphans sent a powerful message of empathy and forgiveness for the tragedies of World War II. Through his vision and leadership, O'Doul had transformed a simple game into a symbol of friendship and cooperation between two nations on the path to reconciliation and mutual respect.

In 1950, the Japanese government acknowledged O'Doul's efforts, with the vice chairman of the Tokyo Metropolitan Board of Education writing to him about the tour's impact on instilling sportsmanship in Japanese youth.[122]

CHAPTER SIX

THE PASTIME THAT SPREAD GOODWILL WITH CUBA AND UKRAINE

The players will be thrilled to visit a country that shares our passion and enthusiasm for the sport of baseball, and we all hope that this visit marks the beginning of a relationship that will only grow stronger—on and off the baseball field.

—Tony Clark, Executive Director of the Major League Baseball Players Association

---

CUBAN TENSIONS

The word *Cuba* evokes different images for different people. For some, Cuba means the Castro Revolution, which rose to power in 1959. For others, Cuba is associated with counterterrorism and immigration. For some, Cuba means vacationing in the sun. These divergent images represent the United States' fluctuating policies toward Cuba. Since Cuba's independence in 1902, U.S. policies toward Cuba have been based on a variety of factors, including Cuba's proximity to the United States, the nature of the government in power, and the fear that other nations will share Cuba's revolutionary ideas.

This fear started on January 1, 1959, when Fidel Castro led a revolution that ousted the Cuban dictator, Fulgencio Batista, and formed a new government with ties to the Soviet Union. The U.S. government, alarmed by the spread of communism so close to its shores, viewed Cuba as a significant threat to democracy.[123] An unsuccessful attempt by the United States to overthrow Castro's regime in 1961, known as the Bay of Pigs Invasion, further deteriorated relations to a full severance.[124] In 1962, the famous Cuban Missile Crisis, which followed the discovery of Soviet missiles in Cuba, cemented Cuba's adversarial position in U.S. foreign policy.

Policy conflicts soon led to the United States launching its first of many sanctions against Cuba, which expanded over the years to include nearly all forms of trade, travel, and financial transactions. Under President Jimmy Carter in 1977, there were brief, direct talks between the two countries, leading to Fidel Castro freeing a handful of political prisoners, while Carter eased travel restrictions for American citizens going to Cuba, as well as the establishment of Interests Sections in Havana and Washington, D.C.[125] However, normalization efforts stalled due to continued ideological differences and geopolitical tensions. After 1991 and the collapse of the Soviet Union, the U.S. embargo left Cuba economically and politically isolated. The United States tightened the embargo with the 1992 Cuba Democracy Act and the 1996 Helms-Burton Act, both aimed to further pressure the Cuban government toward democratic reform and human rights improvements.

Subsequent administrations made various attempts to engage with Cuba in the late 1990s and early 2000s, primarily by easing some travel restrictions, but the fundamental embargo remained in place. By the twenty-first century, the longstanding trade ban had inflicted significant economic hardship on the Cuban population without achieving its intended political goals. The policy had also marginalized the United States from other Latin American countries and global allies who favored engagement over isolation. The rise of China and Venezuela as alternative influences in Latin America gave the United States an incentive to re-engage with Cuba to maintain its regional dominance, with bipartisan support and public opinion, especially among younger generations, growing for reevaluating America's approach to Cuba. The Cuban-American community, once staunchly opposed to the Castro Regime, saw a growing generation in Cuba less wedded to past grievances. Fidel Castro stepped down as President in 2008, succeeded by his brother Raúl, who began showing signs of economic reform, opening up the private sector to a limited extent. American businesses also saw potential economic opportunities in a newly opened Cuban market; this signaled a potential willingness for Cuba to engage with the United States. All these factors, along with the reduction of communist threats to the United States, motivated President Obama to consider a policy shift.

On December 17, 2014, President Obama and President

Raúl Castro simultaneously announced the beginning of a process to normalize relations. Obama eased some travel and trade restrictions, allowing more Americans to visit Cuba and permitting some commercial and financial transactions. In July 2015, the United States and Cuba reopened their embassies, formally restoring diplomatic relations for the first time in over half a century.

2015 MLB GOODWILL TOUR

In December 2015, MLB embarked on a groundbreaking goodwill tour to Cuba. Arranged by Antonio Castro—Fidel Castro's son and the vice president of Cuba's International Baseball Federation, the tour was a carefully orchestrated attempt to bridge the political and cultural differences between the two countries through the shared love of baseball. It followed President Obama's announcement of normalized relations between the United States and Cuba.

One of the tour's most significant aspects was the participation of four Cuban defectors—Yasiel Puig, Jose Abreu, Alexei Ramirez, and Brayan Peña—who returned home to give instructional clinics to over 300 schoolchildren. The Cuban-born players were greeted as celebrities by most Cubans.[126] For these men, the emotional highlight was reuniting with families they hadn't seen in years.

Another highlight was visiting Havana's Esquina Caliente, or "Hot Corner," a historic gathering place where Cubans have long congregated to discuss baseball and politics. With the statue of the Cuban national hero Jose Marti in the background, players engaged in friendly chats with locals, sharing stories and debating the strengths of baseball in their respective countries. Players also participated in youth baseball clinics, connecting with young Cuban athletes and sharing their knowledge of and passion for the game. The visit was particularly meaningful for Cuban-born players, who were able to immerse themselves in their homeland's baseball culture.

Beyond the on-field activities, the tour provided an opportunity for dialogue about the significant obstacles that still remained between the two countries. The U.S. trade embargo, which had been in place since 1960, presented a significant hurdle. Another crucial issue was finding a safe and legal path for Cuban players to join the MLB, as opposed to making dangerous defections. Both the Cuban Baseball Federation and MLB officials expressed a desire to work together toward solutions, hoping to give young athletes the opportunity to pursue their passion without risking the dangers of human trafficking and defection. Dan Halem, MLB's legal chief, acknowledged the unsustainability of the existing system in which Cuban players had to illegally defect to play in the Majors, while Antonio Castro echoed this sentiment.[127]

The tour laid the groundwork for future collaboration between the MLB and Cuba. Plans for Spring Training games in Havana were made, offering opportunities for American teams to engage with Cuban fans and players on their home turf. This possibility, along with the goodwill tour's success, hinted at a brighter future for Cuban baseball, potentially integrating it more seamlessly into the global baseball scene.

By leveraging the transnational appeal of baseball, the 2015 MLB goodwill tour represented a significant milestone in U.S.-Cuba relations, as it coincided with the one-year anniversary of President Obama's move toward normalizing relations with Cuba. Now, talks between MLB and Cuban officials have become more frequent and substantive, with discussions ranging from staging exhibition games in Cuba to the possibility of a regular-season game in the summer. While the tour was a significant first step, both MLB officials and Cuban representatives emphasized that it was just the beginning of a long journey toward normalization. The tour highlighted baseball's significance as a unifying force; as MLB's Chief Baseball Officer Joe Torre said, the experience was "exhilarating" and exceeded all expectations in its positivity and impact.[128]

2022 UKRAINIAN GOODWILL MISSION TO NEW YORK CITY

Ukraine was part of the Soviet Union from 1922 until its independence in 1991. The transition to independence was marked by economic challenges and political instability. Further, the 2004 Ukraine presidential election, marred by widespread allegations of fraud, sparked massive protests in what became known as the Orange Revolution. Viktor Yushchenko, the pro-Western candidate, faced off against the incumbent Prime Minister Viktor Yanukovych, who was seen as pro-Russian. The peaceful protests led to an overturning of the election, resulting in Yushchenko's victory. However, Yanukovych was still elected following the 2010 presidential election. In November 2013, President Yanukovych's decision to suspend the signing of an association agreement with the European Union in favor of fostering closer ties with Russia sparked widespread protests, known as the Euromaidan movement. The protests, demanding closer integration with Europe and an end to corruption, culminated in February 2014 with Yanukovych fleeing the country. This revolution led to a change in government and a clear pivot toward the West. The conflict between Ukraine and Russia escalated dramatically in 2014 when Russia annexed Crimea, a move widely condemned by the international community. Pro-Russian separatists in the Donbas region (comprising Donetsk and Luhansk) declared independence, leading to an ongoing conflict. Despite several ceasefire agreements, including the Minsk Protocols, the situation has remained volatile.[129]

Throughout 2021, there were significant reports of Russian military buildup along the Ukrainian border, raising concerns about an imminent large-scale invasion. On February 24, 2022, Russian President Vladimir Putin announced a "special military operation" in Ukraine, ostensibly to "demilitarize and denazify" the country. This marked the largest attack on a European country since World War II and the beginning of a full-scale invasion, with Russian forces launching attacks on multiple fronts, including from Belarus in the north, Crimea in the south, and Russia in the east. Ukrainian armed forces, bolstered by civilian volunteers, mounted a fierce resistance. The defense of Kyiv, in particular, was notable for its effectiveness in repelling Russian advances and preventing the capture of the capital. The resilience of Ukrainian forces and the leadership of President Volodymyr Zelenskyy, who chose to remain in Kyiv, garnered international admiration and support. Zelenskyy's regular addresses and appeals for global assistance played a crucial role in maintaining morale in and securing aid for his country.[130]

The United States has provided billions of dollars in military aid to Ukraine, including advanced weaponry such as anti-tank missiles, artillery systems, drones, and air-defense systems. In addition, the United States has provided training for Ukrainian forces and shared critical intelligence to improve their operational effectiveness on the battlefield. The United States has offered substantial economic assistance—direct financial aid, loans, and support for infrastructure reconstruction—to help stabilize the Ukrainian economy, which has been severely affected by the war. The United States has also contributed significant humanitarian aid to address the needs of displaced populations and those affected by the conflict, providing food, medical supplies, and shelter. Lastly, the United States has been a vocal advocate for Ukraine in international forums, working to rally global support against Russian aggression. This includes leading efforts at the United Nations and other international bodies to impose sanctions on Russia and isolate it diplomatically.

The human cost of the war has been immense, with tens of thousands of civilians perished, hundreds of thousands more displaced, and multiple cities left in ruins. International response to the conflict has been critical, and diplomatic efforts continue, but a lasting peace deal remains elusive. However, the Ukrainian people have refused to succumb to despair. Instead, they have sought ways to reach out to the world, one being the Ukrainian National Baseball Team's October 2022 goodwill mission to New York City. As the players stepped onto the baseball field of Maimonides Park, in the Coney Island neighborhood of Brooklyn, they carried with them the hopes and dreams of a nation torn apart by conflict, serving as ambassadors of unity in a troubled world.

Two primary objectives drove the Ukrainian team's goodwill journey to New York City: building support through charity games and displaying symbols of resilience. The team participated in two charity games hosted by the Brooklyn Cyclones, facing off against the New York Police Department (NYPD) and the Fire Department of New York (FDNY) baseball teams. The proceeds from these events were earmarked for rebuilding sports facilities in Ukraine, offering tangible assistance to a nation in desperate need. Each swing of the bat and each skillful catch became a symbolic act of reconstruction, a promise of rebuilding buildings, schools, and playgrounds, as well as instilling a sense of normalcy for a nation at war. More than athletic competition, these games were about solidarity and support. Ukrainian head coach Oleg Boyko presented an honorary team jersey to New York City Mayor Eric Adams, stating, "[T]his is a jersey from the national team of Ukraine." Adams replied, "This team behind us has shown the resiliency of what it is to continue to push forward despite all that you are facing."[131]

Perhaps the most profound aspect of the Ukrainian team's mission was the emotional impact it had on both players and spectators alike. For the players, the trip was a chance to connect with fellow human beings who understood their struggle. Ukrainian pitcher Andrii Boiko eloquently captured the sentiment, "Biggest experience that I had here is that many people care about us, they support us. Emotional support is very important."[132] In a world torn apart by conflict and division, the simple act of coming together on a baseball field served as a powerful reminder of our shared humanity.

The Ukrainian team also received a hero's welcome at Yankee Stadium, where they attended a playoff game in the electrifying atmosphere of one of baseball's most iconic venues. This experience carried a responsibility that the players embraced with pride and humility. The highlight of the goodwill mission, however, was the charity games held at Maimonides Park. The free tickets to these games further underscored the mission's true spirit—unity and goodwill.[133] The Ukrainian National Baseball Team's goodwill mission to New York City in 2022 showed us that moments of unity often emerge from the most unexpected places in the face of global turmoil.

Chapter Seven

The Hockey Series That Melted the Ice of the Cold War

Every one of us guys, thirty-five guys that came out and played for Team Canada, we did it because we love our country and not for any other reason, no other reason. They can throw the money for the pension fund out the window. They can throw anything they want out the window. We came because we love Canada.

—Phil Esposito on the 1972 Summit Series, dubbed "Canada's Greatest Speech"[134]

CANADA IN THE COLD WAR

The Cold War, a prolonged period of geopolitical tension and ideological conflict between the U.S.-led Western Bloc and the U.S.S.R.-led Eastern Bloc, shaped much of the mid-twentieth century world. While the narrative is often dominated by the rivalry between the United States and the Soviet Union, Canada, geographically positioned between the two superpowers, played a crucial role in the Western alliance.

The defeat of Nazi Germany and Imperial Japan in 1945 left the United States and the Soviet Union as the world's dominant military powers. Despite the two countries being allies during the war, their relationship quickly soured due to contrasting visions for the post-war order, highlighted by the conferences held in Yalta and Potsdam.[135] Following World War II, the world emerged as a bipolar system. The United States, championing capitalism, democracy, and individual liberty, formed the core of the Western Bloc. Canada, closely aligned with the United States in terms of political and economic systems, became a staunch supporter of the West's ideals; both countries believed in the spread of democracy and free markets as the path to prosperity and stability. While the United States and its allies, including Canada, pushed for democratic governments and free markets in Europe, the Soviet Union sought to establish a buffer zone of friendly Communist states in Eastern Europe to protect against future invasions. This move triggered a sense of encirclement in the West, particularly Canada. The proximity of the Soviet Union to Canada across the Arctic Ocean heightened anxieties about potential aggression.[136]

At the heart of the Cold War was an ideological battle between capitalism, represented by the United States and its Western allies, and communism, embodied by the Soviet Union. Winston Churchill's famous 1946 speech in Fulton, Missouri, declared that an "Iron Curtain" had descended across Europe, symbolizing the division between the democratic West and the communist East. Capitalism advocated for free markets, private property, and democratic governance, while communism promoted state control of the economy, collective ownership, and a one-party state. Canada's robust economy contributed to the Western Bloc's overall strength. Through initiatives like the Marshall Plan, Canada supported European reconstruction, which was essential for building a strong, democratic Europe to counter Soviet influence.[137]

In 1949, Canada became a founding member of the North Atlantic Treaty Organization (NATO), committing to mutual defense against potential Soviet aggression. The creation of NATO formalized the military alliance between the United States, Canada, and other Western European nations. NATO served as a deterrent against Soviet aggression and a symbol of Western solidarity. Canada played a significant role in NATO's defense strategy, contributing troops and participating in joint military exercises. Geographically, Canada's proximity to the Arctic and its extensive coastline made it a strategic ally in the North Atlantic. In 1957, Canada and the United States established the North American Aerospace Defense Command (NORAD) to coordinate continental air defense. During the Cuban Missile Crisis, Canada's NORAD commitments and close military ties with the United States placed it on high alert. Canada supported the U.S. naval blockade of Cuba and contributed to the overall Western stance against Soviet nuclear deployment in the Western Hemisphere.[138]

During this period, the Soviet blockade of West Berlin aimed to force the Western allies out of the city. The Western response and Canada's participation in the Berlin Airlift—sending food and fuel to Berlin from airbases in West Germany due to a Soviet land blockade—demonstrated the resolve to support democratic enclaves within Soviet-controlled areas. Germany's division into democratic West Germany and communist East Germany became a focal point of the Cold War, with Canada supporting the economic and political stability of West Germany as a bulwark against Soviet expansion.

Another example of direct military confrontation between communism and capitalism is the Korean War. During the conflict, Canada contributed significantly to the United Nations forces, fighting alongside American, British, and South Korean troops to repel the North Korean invasion backed by China and the Soviet Union. During the Vietnam War, Canada did not directly participate, but they did play a role in diplomatic efforts and peacekeeping. Canada's position as a non-combatant allowed it to act as an intermediary, particularly during the International Control Commission's monitoring of the 1954 Geneva Accords in which diplomats and military personnel from Canada were responsible for the observance of ceasefires between North and South Vietnam.[139]

The Cold War also had an impact on societal values in

North America. The fear of communist infiltration led to the rise of McCarthyism in the United States and a similar wave of anti-communist sentiment in Canada. Civil liberties were curtailed, and dissent was viewed with suspicion. Canada experienced its own version of the Red Scare, with security measures to root out suspected communist sympathizers within its borders. In 1946, Igor Gouzenko, a Soviet cipher clerk, defected to Ottawa and exposed a Soviet spy ring operating in Canada. This event heightened awareness of the communist threat and reinforced Canada's commitment to the Western alliance.[140]

In the 1970s, the period of detente saw efforts to ease tensions between the United States and the Soviet Union. Canada played a role in international diplomacy, advocating for arms control agreements like the Strategic Arms Limitation Talks (SALT).[141] Canada's foreign policy emphasized human rights, aligning with Western efforts to highlight the Soviet Union's repressive policies and lack of political freedoms.

With its superior economic resources, the Western Bloc maintained sustained pressure on the Soviet Union. Canada's economic strength also contributed to the overall Western strategy of outpacing Soviet economic capabilities. The arms and space races were key components of the Cold War competition, and Canadian scientists and engineers participated in Western technological advancements, including contributions to space exploration through collaboration with NASA.

By the 1980s, the Soviet Union faced severe economic difficulties and political unrest. The USSR leader Mikhail Gorbachev's policies of glasnost (openness) and perestroika (restructuring) aimed to reform the system but also exposed its weaknesses.[142] Western leaders, including Canada, supported movements for democratic reforms within the Eastern Bloc. Canada's diplomatic efforts and support for human rights played a role in the broader strategy to encourage Soviet liberalization.

HOCKEY DIPLOMACY

The 1972 Summit Series between Canada and the Soviet Union was a cultural and political phenomenon. Played during the Cold War and with four games in each country, this eight-game battle on the ice between Team Canada and Team Soviet Union unexpectedly became a catalyst for a cautious thaw in relations between the two countries. In the aftermath, diplomatic channels opened, paving the way for increased cultural exchanges and people-to-people connections.

Prior to the Summit Series, Canada and the Soviet Union existed in a state of political and cultural isolation from each other, separated by the Iron Curtain. Hockey, however, provided an unlikely bridge; the series captivated audiences on both sides, showcasing athletic skills and glimpses of each other's cultures. At the end of the 1960s, the USSR and Canada were dominant forces in hockey but didn't participate in much international competition. The idea of meetups between the two was initiated by Sergei Pavlov, the chairman of the State Committee for Physical Culture and Sports of the USSR. The Canadian embassy in Moscow soon picked up on the Soviets' interest, and plans were finalized at the 1972 World Ice Hockey Championships. As mentioned before, both sides agreed to play four games in Canada and four games in the

Soviet Union under international rules.

Led by the seasoned National Hockey League (NHL) coach Harry Sinden, Team Canada—assembled from NHL stars—was a formidable force comprised of some of the greatest players ever to lace up their skates. From the legendary goaltending of the young Ken Dryden to the offensive prowess of Phil Esposito, the league's leading scorer, Team Canada boasted a roster overflowing with talent and experience. Other offensive threats included Bobby Hull, who ultimately didn't play due to signing with the rival World Hockey Association; Frank Mahovlich; and Dryden. Four co-captains were named: Esposito, Stan Mikita, Mahovlich, and Jean Ratelle. This leadership structure aimed to leverage the experience and respect these veterans commanded within the locker room.[143]

Team Canada assembled in Toronto for a training camp in August 1972. However, their preparation for the series was hindered by several factors, including their unfamiliarity with the Soviet system of play, coupled with the loss of key players like Bobby Hull. Additionally, due to the subjectivity of Sinden's thirty-five-man roster, the team lacked the cohesion of a traditional national team that played together regularly; many players were also past their prime or lacked international experience. The series witnessed the rise of unexpected heroes. The unheralded line of Bobby Clarke, Ron Ellis, and Paul Henderson, not projected initially to start, impressed in camp and played a pivotal role throughout the series, with Henderson scoring the series-winning goals in Game 8.[144]

The 1972 Summit Series wasn't just about Canada's all-star team; it was also a showcase for the dominant Soviet national team, the well-oiled "Red Machine." Unlike Team Canada, which, you recall, had been assembled with established NHL stars, the Soviet team was a product of the country's systematic approach to player development. From a young age, promising players were identified and trained within a national program emphasizing teamwork, discipline, and a structured system of play.[145]

The Soviet roster boasted its own collection of talented players: Valeri Kharlamov, nicknamed the "Soviet Gretzky," dazzled with his offensive skills; Vladislav Tretiak, a young and acrobatic goaltender, emerged as a series MVP contender; and veterans like Alexander Yakushev and Vladimir Petrov provided leadership and offensive powers.[146] But the Soviets' greatest strength wasn't individual talent; it was their cohesive team play. Their system emphasized quick puck movement, cycling the puck through the offensive zone, and a relentless forecheck. This tactical approach initially surprised and frustrated Team Canada, who were accustomed to a more individualistic style of play.[147] The Soviet team presented a unique challenge compared to traditional Canadian competitors, forcing Team Canada to adapt their strategies accordingly.

The series kicked off in Montreal, Canada, on September 2, 1972, in an atmosphere of unparalleled anticipation and excitement. The series opener at the Montreal Forum was a rude awakening for a Canadian team brimming with confidence. Despite scoring the first two goals, Team Canada found themselves outmatched by the speed, discipline, and tactical brilliance of the Soviet squad. Kharlamov put on a dazzling display, scoring a goal and assisting on three others as the Soviets secured a convincing 7-3 victory. The game exposed the weaknesses of the aging Canadian roster and their lack of preparation for the Soviet system of play.[148] The Soviet team, composed of highly skilled and disciplined players, stunned the Canadian crowd by taking an early lead in the series.

The series shifted to Toronto for Game 2, where Canada sought a comeback in front of a raucous hometown crowd. Facing public outcry after the Game 1 defeat, Team Canada responded with a more determined effort. Esposito ignited the home crowd with a hat trick, and Canada managed to hold on for a 4-1 victory. While the win didn't erase the earlier loss, it was a morale booster and demonstrated Canada's ability to compete.

The series shifted to Winnipeg for Game 3. Canada raced to a lead, but the Soviets battled back with two shorthanded goals, including one from the young star Kharlamov. The game ended in a dramatic 4-4 tie, the only draw of the series. While Canada regretted overconfidence, the Soviets complained about officiating and physical play, highlighting the growing tension amid and competitiveness of the Summit Series.

In a disappointing turn for Canadian fans, Game 4 in Vancouver saw Team Canada fall 5-3 to the Soviets. Bill Goldsworthy's early penalties gifted the Soviets two power-play goals by Boris Mikhailov, putting Canada on the back foot from the start. Gilbert Perreault managed to get one past Vladislav Tretiak in the second, but Yuri Blinov quickly responded. A controversial disallowed goal by Rod Gilbert, which Coach Sinden believed could have changed the game's trajectory, further dampened Canadian spirits. Vladimir Vikulov extended the Soviet lead before Goldsworthy and Hull scored consolation goals in the third. Despite these efforts, Dryden's shaky performance in the net couldn't match Tretiak's brilliance, and the Soviets secured a convincing victory. This loss, coupled with lineup changes that didn't pay off, left Coach Sinden feeling the pressure as the series headed to Moscow. The frustrated Canadians crowd booed their own team off the ice.

Team Canada arrived in Moscow for Game 5 in a tense atmosphere. Canada stormed to a 3-0 lead with goals from Jean-Paul Parisé, Clarke, and Henderson. The Soviets fought back in the third, however. Blinov and Vikulov scored, followed by a defensive lapse from Canada that allowed the Soviets Vyacheslav Anisin and Vladimir Shadrin to net goals. The final blow came from Vikulov, securing a stunning 5-4 Soviet victory and a commanding 3-1-1 series lead. Despite the crushing defeat, Canadian fans sang "O Canada" in a show of solidarity, surprising Soviet observers. Now facing an uphill battle with Perreault's departure, Team Canada needed a miracle to win the series.

Canada pulled off a crucial win in Game 6, leading 3-1 early in the second period and eventually holding on for a 3-2 victory. A goal by Henderson proved to be the game winner.

In a critical Game 7, Coach Sinden employed a new four-line formation—a strategy that involves utilizing players with strong physical abilities to provide defense while those with scoring potential rest—to counter the Soviets' defensive tactics against Phil Esposito. This gamble paid off as Canada emerged victorious, 4-3. Esposito's two goals in the first period were matched by Yakushev and Petrov for the Soviets. After a scoreless second period, Gilbert put Canada ahead, but Yakushev tied it again. The game-winning moment came late in the third with Henderson's controversial goal. He fooled a Soviet defender, skated around him, and scored on Tretiak. Though Henderson was tripped by a Soviet player, the goal stood, sparking celebration and leaving the Soviets to publicly blame the loss on a defensive mistake. This dramatic victory evened the series at 3-3-1, setting the stage for a thrilling final game.

Despite consecutive wins in games 6 and 7, Canada knew they needed to win Game 8 to secure victory. Tensions quickly escalated when controversial penalties led to an early goal by Yakushev. Things reached a boiling point when Parisé received a questionable penalty and reacted by angrily charging the referee with his stick. This sparked outrage from the crowd, who chanted, "Let's go home," seemingly ready to abandon the game. However, team management decided to continue, and ironically, Parisé's outburst seemed to fire up the Canadian team for the crucial final match. After the second period ended, the Soviets led 5-3. With hope still high, Esposito scored with 2:27 left in the third period. Then, after another goal for Canada by Yvan Cournoyer, the Soviets were ready to claim the series victory off an extra goal on aggregate. But with just 34 seconds remaining, it was Paul Henderson who etched his name into hockey lore, scoring the game-winning goal that clinched victory for Team Canada and secured their place in history. It was a moment of pure joy and national pride as Canadians from coast to coast erupted in celebration of their team's triumph.[149]

MELTING THE ICE OF COLD WAR

At the heart of the Summit Series was the clash between two contrasting ideologies: the capitalist democracy of Canada and the communist regime of the Soviet Union. The games were not merely about goals and victories on the ice but represented a microcosm of the broader East-West tensions that defined the Cold War era. Each game became a battleground for supremacy in hockey and ideological dominance, with both nations vying to prove the superiority of their respective political system.

The significance of the Summit Series lay not only in its geopolitical implications but also in its ability to captivate the hearts and minds of people on both sides of the Iron Curtain. In Canada, the series ignited a sense of national pride and unity as citizens rallied behind their team in a display of patriotism rarely seen before. The games became a unifying force, transcending regional, linguistic, and cultural divides to bring together Canadians from coast to coast in support of a common cause. Similarly, in the Soviet Union, the Summit Series took on immense significance as a showcase of the prowess of Soviet sport and the achievements of the Communist system. Hockey, often considered Canada's national game, allowed the Soviet Union to demonstrate its athletic prowess and challenge the perception of Western superiority in sports. The success of the Soviet team in the early games of the series sparked celebrations across the nation and bolstered national pride at a time of heightened international tensions.

However, beyond the fervor of national pride and sporting glory, the Summit Series also catalyzed diplomatic engagement between Canada and the Soviet Union. According to Boris Mikhailov, who scored in Game 3 of the series, "[It] was a meeting between two schools of hockey, and we have since continued this great exchange and we have learned from each other, taking the best of both styles."[150] The interactions between players, coaches, and officials from both teams encouraged a degree of cultural exchange and mutual understanding beyond political differences. While the series was marked by intense competition and occasional controversy, it also provided opportunities for dialogue and cooperation between adversaries on the ice.

The games were played at a time when the world always seemed on the brink of a nuclear war, and tensions between Canada and the Soviet Union were at an all-time high. The hockey games connected two nations locked in a tense political rivalry and also helped break down some of the barriers and stereotypes between Canadians and Russians. Many Canadians had viewed the Soviets as cold, calculating, and unfeeling, while many Russians had viewed the Canadians as arrogant and self-centered. The hockey games helped to dispel these myths and showed that people on both sides were capable of great passion, dedication, and sportsmanship. For the first time, Canadian media offered extensive coverage of Soviet life. Beyond the hockey rink, audiences witnessed images of cheering Soviet fans, humanizing these citizens from a previously demonized nation. Similarly, Soviet audiences were exposed to the fast-paced, physical style of Canadian hockey and the passionate Canadian fan culture. This newfound familiarity created a sense of understanding that transcended political rhetoric.

Beyond the goals and victories, the series served as a mirror reflecting the broader geopolitical dynamics of the Cold War era. In the aftermath of the series, diplomatic channels that had long been frozen began to thaw. The success of the series, completed without major political incidents, served as a confidence booster for further diplomatic efforts. Both nations recognized the potential of sports diplomacy. In 1973, just a year after the series concluded, Canada signed the first agreement with the Soviet Union on cultural and scientific exchange. There was a surge in cultural initiatives aimed at mutual understanding and appreciation—cultural delegations, including artists, musicians, and writers, began to travel between the two countries, showcasing their respective talents and traditions.[151] Furthermore, the Summit Series sparked a newfound interest in each other's societies; Canadians became curious about life behind the Iron Curtain, while the Soviets developed a fascination with Canada's open society and freedoms. This curiosity led to a surge in educational exchanges, with students and scholars from both countries seeking opportunities to study abroad and learn about each other's political systems, economies, and cultures.

Unfortunately, despite all this, the Cold War would continue for decades after the final puck dropped in Moscow. Still, the Summit Series is another example for the potential for sports to bridge political divides and establish a sense of shared humanity.

CHAPTER EIGHT

THE RUGBY TOURNAMENT THAT UNITED A NATION

We didn't have 60,000 South Africans; we had 43 million South Africans.

—Francois Pienaar, captain of the 1995 South African rugby team[152]

On June 24, 1995, at Johannesburg's Ellis Park Stadium, South Africa clinched victory over its archrival New Zealand in the Rugby World Cup final, winning 15-12 in a match that became a symbol of national unity. This historic moment marked South Africa's first major sporting event since 1991; the country, fresh from the shackles of apartheid, was hosting the Rugby World Cup. The tournament showcased the masterful statecraft of President Nelson Mandela, who used rugby to foster reconciliation in a deeply divided nation.[153]

APARTHEID IN SOUTH AFRICA

South Africa's racial tensions trace their roots to colonialism. In the seventeenth century, Dutch settlers established a system of racial hierarchy in South Africa that privileged whites. British colonization in the nineteenth century solidified these divisions, culminating in 1910 in the creation of the Union of South Africa, a state built on white supremacy.[154] Both colonial powers imposed systems of racial segregation and exploitation of indigenous African populations and imported slaves.

After gaining independence from British rule, the Union of South Africa continued institutionalized racial discrimination through laws such as the Natives (not Black) Land Act of 1913, which restricted Black landownership. In 1948, the National Party, which had come to power in 1914, formally instituted apartheid as a policy of rigid racial segregation and white supremacy. The cornerstone laws included the Population Registration Act, Group Areas Act, and the Bantu Education Act, which segregated public spaces, divided the country into areas based on race, and denied Black South Africans the right to vote. This system severely limited Black access to education, healthcare, and economic opportunities.[155]

Founded in 1912, the African National Congress (ANC) was the most prominent voice against apartheid.[156] While the ANC initially advocated for peaceful protest, it hardened its stance after the Sharpeville Massacre in 1960, in which police opened fire on unarmed protestors, killing sixty-nine people. The massacre galvanized international condemnation and increased internal resistance, leading to the South African government's banning the ANC and other anti-apartheid organizations.[157]

A young lawyer, Nelson Mandela, became a crucial figure in the resistance. He co-founded the militant Umkhonto we Sizwe (Spear of the Nation, or MK for short) in 1961, launching an armed struggle against the apartheid regime. MK carried out sabotage campaigns against government installations to weaken the apartheid regime. As a result, Mandela was arrested in 1962 and subsequently tried at the Rivonia Trial, where he delivered his famous "I am prepared to die" speech.[158] In 1964, he was sentenced to life imprisonment. Mandela's incarceration on Robben Island, where he endured harsh conditions and forced labor, became a global symbol of the anti-apartheid struggle. Despite limited communication, his writings and statements inspired activists worldwide.

Soon, the Free Nelson Mandela campaign gained momentum, with increasing calls from international leaders, organizations, and ordinary citizens for his release. Economic sanctions and cultural boycotts put significant pressure on the apartheid regime. The Soweto Uprising of 1976, in which Black students protested against the imposition of Afrikaans as a medium of instruction, drew further global attention to the brutality of apartheid. Internally, within South Africa, white dissent against apartheid grew. The detention of anti-apartheid activists like Winnie Mandela, Nelson's wife, and the death of Black activist Steve Biko due to brain injuries incurred during security-police detention sparked continued outrage. Many Afrikaners began to question the morality and sustainability of the apartheid system. By the late 1980s, the tide began to turn. President F.W. de Klerk, recognizing the international pressure and internal dissent, took steps to dismantle apartheid. In 1990, he legalized the ANC and other banned organizations and, most importantly, released Nelson Mandela after Mandela had spent twenty-seven years in prison.[159]

Mandela's release was a watershed moment. He emerged as a powerful symbol of reconciliation and forgiveness, advocating for a negotiated settlement rather than continued violence. He and President de Klerk embarked on a series of talks, culminating in the Codesa (Convention for a Democratic South Africa) negotiations that laid the groundwork for an interim constitution adopted in 1993 and for South Africa's first multiracial elections in April 1994. The ANC won a majority, and Nelson Mandela was inaugurated as the country's first Black president on May 10, 1994.[160]

Mandela prioritized national healing and reconciliation. The Truth and Reconciliation Commission, chaired by Archbishop Desmond Tutu, was established to address the human rights violations of the apartheid era. Mandela's administration focused on creating an inclusive government, promoting racial harmony, and addressing socioeconomic inequalities through policies such as the Reconstruction and Development Program, which contributed to more housing, cleaner water, and new healthcare in the twenty-first century. Mandela's moral authority and statesmanship earned him global respect. In 1993, Mandela and F.W. de Klerk were jointly awarded the Nobel Peace Prize for their efforts in peacefully ending apartheid and laying the foundations for a democratic South Africa.[161] The end of apartheid had not been a singular event but was the culmination of decades of struggle by the

Black South African majority and their allies. Still, despite the dismantling of apartheid, South Africa continues to grapple with the inequalities it left in its wake.

RUGBY DIPLOMACY

Before it ended, apartheid's gross human-rights violations had long made South Africa an international pariah, with the United Nations in 1974 declaring apartheid a "crime against humanity."[162] The racially segregated policies of apartheid extended even to sports, with South Africa facing international bans from events like the Olympic Games and the Rugby World Cup due to its discriminatory practices. The 1995 Rugby World Cup would thus be the stage for Mandela's vision of a united South Africa to make its global debut—the sport, historically dominated by white South Africans and symbolizing the nation's oppressive minority white rule, became a focal point for Mandela's efforts to bridge the racial divide.

Recognizing the sport's potential to foster unity, Mandela orchestrated a campaign of reconciliation centered on the slogan "One Team, One Country." His vision wasn't without its challenges. Black South Africans resented the national rugby team's Springbok emblem, the mascot associated with apartheid. Yet, Mandela understood the importance of Afrikaner identity, deeply intertwined with the team. Disbanding the Springboks, he reasoned, would only deepen the chasm and Mandela in fact appeared at Ellis Park during the World Cup wearing the Springbok green.

The sight of Mandela embracing rugby, a sport long considered a bastion of white privilege, sent a powerful message of inclusivity and reconciliation. Before the final against New Zealand, a new national anthem—a blend of the Afrikaans "Die Stem" and the anti-apartheid hymn "Nkosi Sikelel' iAfrika"—rang out across the stadium. When Mandela walked onto the field in the Springboks jersey, the predominantly Afrikaner crowd erupted in cheers of "Nelson, Nelson, Nelson!"

Furthermore, Mandela's outreach to François Pienaar, the team's captain, demonstrated a commitment to interacting with both Black and white communities. Mandela and Pienaar had tea in his office at the Union Buildings in Pretoria and talked many times during pre-World Cup training sessions in Cape Town. Despite initial skepticism and opposition, Mandela's strategic engagement with the rugby establishment paved the way for a historic moment of national unity.

The climax of the 1995 Rugby World Cup final, with South Africa securing victory in a hard-fought contest, was met with jubilation and celebration across the nation. Black and white South Africans alike reveled in the shared triumph, marking a true moment of collective pride and solidarity. While the victory on the rugby field did not erase the deep-rooted injustices of apartheid, it served as hope for a nation in transition. The tournament's most memorable moment unfolded following the game's conclusion, as Mandela, donning a Springbok cap and jersey, presented the Webb Ellis Cup to Pienaar. When asked about the tremendous support from the 65,000 South Africans in the stadium, François Pienaar gave the iconic one-liner that brought a rugby-loving nation together: "We didn't have 60,000 South Africans; we had 43 million South Africans."[163]

However, the legacy of the 1995 Rugby World Cup is complex. Despite Mandela's efforts to use rugby as a catalyst for reconciliation, the national team's failure to fully transform and embrace racial diversity remains a point of contention. From 1996 to 2019, 131 Springboks were chosen from just 25 schools—and 119 of the players were white. The continued dominance of white players within the Springbok ranks reflects broader issues of inequality and exclusion that persist in post-apartheid South Africa. Nevertheless, Mandela's strategic vision and leadership in leveraging sport as a vehicle for social change remain enduring symbols of hope and possibility. As Mandela famously remarked, "Sport has the power to change the world. Sport can create hope, where once there was only despair." Mandela's use of rugby in 1995 wasn't a solution but a potent symbol representing the possibility of national healing, the hope for a future where past divisions would no longer dictate the present.

INTERVIEW WITH CRISTOPHER BALLINAS VALDÉS

Cristopher Ballinas Valdés (DPhil in Politics from Oxford) is an academic, policy maker, and former diplomat who designed Mexico's international policy on human rights and its feminist foreign policy.

Yifei Kevin Niu: *How do you believe sports can play a role in improving and advocating for human rights?*

Cristopher Ballinas Valdés: Sports play a crucial role in advancing human rights. By embracing the principles of respect and fair play, sports teach us important lessons about non-discrimination and inclusivity, demonstrating what equal participation looks like. Additionally, sports challenge stereotypes, helping to dismantle societal barriers and drive progress.

Sports possess a unique and powerful ability to influence and enhance human rights globally. They serve as a platform to raise awareness about human-rights issues, with high-profile athletes and major sporting events attracting significant media attention. This visibility can be leveraged to highlight injustices and advocate for change. For instance, athletes have used their platforms to speak out against racial discrimination, gender inequality, and other critical human-rights concerns. The United Nations High Commissioner for Human Rights has even stated that athletes promoting equality in sports are, in fact, human-rights defenders (UN Human Rights Council 56).

Sports have proven effective in fostering social inclusion by bringing together people from diverse backgrounds, promoting understanding and tolerance. They also have the potential to empower marginalized communities, especially in regions where certain groups face systemic discrimination. Sports can create opportunities for these individuals to participate and thrive, challenging stereotypes and prejudices.

Access to sports programs allows individuals from disadvantaged backgrounds to gain confidence, leadership skills, and a sense of purpose. This empowerment can lead to greater social mobility and help challenge the structures that perpetuate inequality. Moreover, sports foster discussions on fairness and inclusion, addressing both issues simultaneously.

In essence, sports can be a powerful vehicle for positive change, but this potential is realized only when stakeholders are committed and able to include human rights as an action principle into every facet of the sporting world

YKN: *What are some of the challenges or inequalities that athletes face in term of their human rights in sports?*

CBV: Athletes encounter numerous human-rights challenges and inequalities, many of which are deeply rooted in the sports industry. A significant issue is the exploitation of athletes, particularly those who are young or come from vulnerable backgrounds. This exploitation can take the form of unfair contracts, excessive training demands, or inadequate compensation, all of which take advantage of the athlete's labor and talent without providing fair remuneration or protections.

Another major challenge is widespread discrimination and harassment. Despite some progress, issues such as racism, sexism, and homophobia remain prevalent in sports. Female athletes, for example, often receive unequal pay and fewer opportunities compared to their male counterparts, and athletes from racial and ethnic minorities may face systemic biases.

Additionally, LGBTQ+ athletes can experience discrimination and a lack of acceptance, both within their sports and from the fan base, as seen during the Paris Olympics in 2024. On one hand, anti-transgender activists argue that restricting transgender athletes is necessary to protect biological women. On the other hand, transgender-rights defenders assert that transgender athletes must be able to compete in sports in a safe environment. However, behind the rights debate often lie power struggles disguised as well-intentioned actions.

For years, anti-transgender activists have argued that physiological differences between sexes matter in sports. Their lobbying has been intense, leading the NAIA [National Association of Intercollegiate Athletics] to state this week [8/29/24] that sports "include some combination of strength, speed, and stamina, providing competitive advantages for male student-athletes"; therefore, significant physical differences will affect the fairness of "gender-affected sports."

It is then necessary to recognize that sport is not just about competition; it is also a way for people to increase self-development, and no one should be excluded from the fulfilment it provides. Many trans people find in sports a friendly environment for self-expression but often find, in and out of the dressing rooms, the same discriminatory attitudes they typically experience in their daily life. Therefore, banning is not a solution but a way for deepening the problem. To reconcile these conflicting views, we need to transform the discussion of "fair and safe sports" to one of "fair, safe, and dignified sports." The underlying principle of sports is to prove that we can be better humans, not just faster, higher, and stronger.

On a larger scale, international sports organizations have a responsibility to uphold and promote human rights in all aspects of their operations. This includes ensuring that workers involved in the construction of sporting facilities are treated fairly, that events do not contribute to the displacement of communities, and that the principles of equality and non-discrimination are upheld in every aspect of the sport.

Organizations should adopt a human-rights-based approach, especially considering those overcoming adversity to prove themselves in the sports world. This creates larger sporting communities instead of intensifying and deepening social divisions.

YKN: *Is there any collaboration between human-rights organizations and sports organizations? Can you provide examples?*

CBV: There are several [...that have been] crucial in leveraging the influential platform of sports to promote human-rights awareness and advocacy. I have been fortunate to participate in some of these discussions on sports and human rights at the IOC, FIFA, the UN, and in public institutions in my homeland.

One example is the collaboration between the United Nations Human Rights Office and the IOC. They have worked together to promote equality and combat discrimination in sports. This partnership focuses on ensuring that the Olympic Games and related activities uphold the highest standards of human rights, including gender equality, non-discrimination, and the protection of children. The Centre for Sport and Human Rights has also been instrumental in advancing these efforts.

These examples illustrate the growing recognition within the sports world of the importance of human rights. Such collaborations are essential for ensuring that sports not only provide entertainment but also contribute positively to social justice and the betterment of human societies.

CHAPTER NINE

THE FIFA WORLD CUP THAT BROUGHT OUT THE BEST OF IRAN

We did more in ninety minutes than the politicians did in twenty years.

—Jeff Agoo, U.S. defender in the 1998 FIFA World Cup[164]

IRAN AND THE UNITED STATES

While the recent history of U.S.-Iran relations has been marked by political intrigue, revolution, hostage crises, and shifting alliances, the relationship between the two countries in the early twentieth century was relatively cordial. With American missionaries and educators living and working in Iran, the United States was seen as a non-imperial power, unlike Britain and Russia, which had had significant influence in Iran.

In 1941, during World War II, Iran's strategic location led to an Allied invasion to secure oil supplies and a supply route to the Soviet Union. Former Shah of Iran Reza Shah was forced to abdicate, and his son, Mohammad Reza Pahlavi, ascended to the throne. In 1951, Prime Minister Mohammad Mossadegh nationalized Iran's oil industry, which had previously been controlled by the British-owned Anglo-Iranian Oil Company. This move was popular domestically but alarmed Western powers, particularly Britain and the United States. In 1953, the U.S. Central Intelligence Agency (CIA) and the British Secret Intelligence Service (MI6) orchestrated a coup to overthrow Mossadegh and reinstate the Shah. Known as Operation Ajax, this coup was motivated by Cold War dynamics and fears of communist influence in Iran. The coup reinstalled Mohammad Reza Shah as an authoritarian ruler, leading to increased U.S. influence in Iran. The Shah implemented pro-Western policies, receiving substantial American military and economic aid.

The Shah's White Revolution in the 1960s aimed at modernizing and westernizing Iran through land reforms, women's suffrage, and industrial expansion. While these reforms brought economic growth, they also disrupted traditional society and created economic disparities. The Shah's regime became increasingly repressive, using the secret police, SAVAK, to silence opposition. This repression fueled resentment among various social groups, including the clergy, intellectuals, and students. Among the Shah's critics was Ayatollah Ruhollah Khomeini, an influential cleric who opposed the regime's secular and pro-Western policies. Exiled in 1964, Khomeini continued to inspire opposition from abroad, advocating for an Islamic government.

In 1978, Iran's economic woes, political repression, and cultural discontent culminated in widespread protests. The Shah's inability to quell the unrest led to his departure from Iran in January 1979. Shortly thereafter, Khomeini returned from exile, becoming the leader of the Islamic Revolution. In April 1979, a national referendum established the Islamic Republic of Iran, with Khomeini as the Supreme Leader. The new government was characterized by anti-Western rhetoric and policies. In November 1979, Iranian militants seized the U.S. Embassy in Tehran, taking 52 American diplomats and citizens hostage. The hostage crisis lasted 444 days, profoundly affecting U.S.-Iran relations. The United States attempted a rescue mission in April 1980, resulting in failure and further humiliation. The hostages were finally released on January 20, 1981, the day Ronald Reagan was inaugurated as President.

Shortly after the hostage crisis, Iraq invaded Iran, initiating a brutal eight-year conflict. The United States, along with other Western nations, provided support to Iraq, viewing it as a counterbalance to the revolutionary Iranian regime. The war devastated Iran's economy and infrastructure, leading to significant loss of life and further entrenching anti-American sentiment among Iranians, who perceived U.S. support for Iraq as direct aggression. Following the Iran-Iraq War, the United States adopted a "dual containment" policy aimed at limiting the influence of both Iran and Iraq in the Persian Gulf. Economic sanctions were imposed on Iran, further straining bilateral relations.

Since the 1979 hostage crisis, the United States and Iran have had no formal diplomatic relations. Attempts at rapprochement were undermined by mutual distrust and opposing geopolitical interests. Throughout the 1980s and 1990s, the United States imposed various economic sanctions on Iran, targeting its oil industry and financial institutions to pressure the Iranian government to change its policies. Both nations developed negative stereotypes of each other. In the United States, Iran was often portrayed as a rogue state sponsoring terrorism. In Iran, the United States was depicted as the "Great Satan," an imperialist power intent on undermining Iranian sovereignty.

SOCCER DIPLOMACY

The 1998 Fédération Internationale de Football Association (FIFA) World Cup in France drew Iran and the United States into the same group, setting the stage for a highly anticipated match that June 21. Given the historical enmity, the match was to be a diplomatic encounter on the global stage, providing a rare opportunity for positive engagement between the two nations. Anticipation and tension began to build from the moment the draw for the World Cup placed the United States and Iran in Group F. The president of the U.S. Soccer Federation, Alan Rothenberg, aptly called it "the mother of all games," reflecting the magnitude of the encounter.[165] However, for the political regime in Tehran, the prospect of facing off against the United States was met with trepidation. The clash drew a global audience, even those with no interest in the sport. Despite the political backdrop, both teams were to play with determination and commendable sportsmanship, earning a Fair Play award from FIFA.[166]

In the days leading up to the game, tensions were palpable, fueled by a series of events that underscored the deep-seated animosity between the two nations. A week prior to the scheduled kickoff, French television aired the American movie *Not Without My Daughter,* relating the story of an American woman and her daughter escaping her abusive husband in Iran and depicting the harsh realities of life in that country. The film's airing incited outrage in Tehran, with the Iranian embassy considering withdrawing the national team from the World Cup in protest. Supreme Leader Ayatollah Ali Khamenei even threatened to pull Iranian players from the match, citing objections to their shaking hands with the American team and issuing orders that the Iranian team not approach the Americans, posing a direct challenge to FIFA regulations. However, through skillful negotiation, the Iranian-born Mehrdad Masoudi, serving as a FIFA media officer for the match, managed to broker a compromise that saw the Americans approach the Iranians instead, while a referee, Urs Meier from Switzerland, proposed a further sensible solution: instead of the customary pre-match handshakes, the players could pose for a group picture at center field. In a gesture of goodwill, both teams exchanged banners, signaling a temporary truce amidst the political turmoil.

Meanwhile, security measures were intensified to unprecedented levels. FIFA officials reported a tenfold increase in security presence, with 150 armed police officers deployed—a remarkable figure for a World Cup match. This was primarily because intelligence had revealed plans by a terrorist organization to stage a protest during the match: Mujahedin Khalq, an Iraq-based group funded by Saddam Hussein, sought to exploit the occasion to destabilize the Iranian regime. FIFA and security forces worked tirelessly to mitigate the threat, issuing warnings to TV cameramen and implementing enhanced security measures to prevent disruptions.

For its part, Iran adopted a more hawkish stance towards the matchup, driven by the weight of historical grievances. Many families who had lost loved ones in the 1980–1988 Iran-Iraq conflict reached out to the athletes, emphasizing the significance of the match and imploring them to emerge victorious. Forward Khodadad Azizi highlighted the immense pressure on the team, stating, "Many families of martyrs are expecting us to win."[167] The Lyon stadium thus became a stage for a complex interplay of emotions as Iran and the United States came face-to-face through the medium of soccer nearly two decades after diplomatic relations were severed following the storming of the U.S. embassy in Tehran in 1979 and the subsequent 444-day hostage crisis.

Despite these challenges, the match itself unfolded as a way for the athletes to represent their countries. The Iranian Football Federation sought to showcase their country in the best possible light, with players carrying white roses, a symbol of peace, onto the soccer field signaling that the only competition between the two countries would be on the field. In return, the American players presented the Iranian players with U.S. Soccer Federation pennants, and the two squads came together for the aforementioned group photo. Many players, perhaps sensing the historic nature of the occasion, couldn't help but crack a smile. The joint team photo captured the spirit of camaraderie, setting the stage for the historic showdown. "It's just like a sign of like sport trumping politics and all that. That was very important and having the mixed photo was great," Cobi Jones, then a midfielder for the U.S. team, said in the ESPN report.[168]

The game itself was a thriller. Iran, playing with heart, took a commanding lead in the fortieth minute with a header from Hamid Estili. Iran then furthered its lead in the eighty-fourth minute with a counterattack that ended with Mehdi Mahdavikia sliding a low shot past American goalkeeper Kasey Keller. The United States was able to pull a goal back late in the match, but it was too late. In what proved to be a competitive, full-blooded, and fair contest, Iran emerged victorious 2-1, securing their first-ever World Cup victory. For Iranians, it was a validation of their national pride. The Iranian regime, initially apprehensive about the match's implications, found itself confronting the power of sports to unite and inspire. The streets of Tehran erupted in jubilation, with celebrations transcending political divides. Even the Revolutionary Guards, known for their strict enforcement of social codes, found themselves swept up in the euphoria.

For the United States, defeat meant elimination from the World Cup. However, players recognized the profound impact of their participation; as the U.S. defender Jeff Agoos aptly summarized: "We did more in ninety minutes than the politicians did in twenty years."

The impact of the 1998 World Cup match extended beyond the final whistle. Eighteen months later, the

Iranian and U.S. teams met again in a friendly match held in California. While this event, which would have been unthinkable before the France encounter, did not lead to significant diplomatic changes, it was a friendly reminder that we can still view each other through a non-political lens. Through skillful diplomacy, careful planning, and a shared commitment to sportsmanship, FIFA and the participating teams demonstrated the extraordinary power of the World Cup in fostering useful dialogue. In a mere ninety minutes, a soccer game offered a glimmer of hope for a peaceful future. The white roses, the joint photo, and the fierce yet fair competition all contributed to a moment of unity that resonated far beyond the confines of the stadium.

INTERVIEW WITH JOSE LUIS FONT

Jose Luis Font has worked at various companies in the fields of marketing, tourism and travel, and event production, and is currently the Director of Business Development for BEYOND Hospitality. He has participated in the organization of four FIFA World Cups as well forty-plus other sporting events around the world, including the Olympics, Youth Olympics, Pan American Games, NFL Super Bowl, Youth FIFA World Cups, Concacaf Gold Cups, Golf Ryder Cup, and Formula One.

Yifei Kevin Niu: *When planning sports events, how do you navigate and consider political tensions, both locally and globally,* *to ensure the event's success and safety?*

Jose Luis Font: One of the many challenges of organizing major international sporting events is that it's inevitable to come across a host nation that may be facing local or regional political tensions. Our approach, regardless of the capacity in which we are participating in the event's organization, is that safety is always a priority, to ensure that what we are selling, promoting, and/or operating with is done in the best-controlled environment for our clients, guests and, of course, our staff, colleagues, and suppliers.

The first step is always to be duly informed about where it is we're going and what we can expect from the host nation and region in terms of the current political, social, and economic atmosphere. [I also try] to understand a little bit about their history and cultural background so that, whatever hurdles are to be met, we can tackle understanding the context and historic implications.

Since we form part of a big "machinery" (the event in and of itself), the event organizers have a dedicated Security & Safety department that liaises at all times with the local authorities and others to assess any potential risks and determine a correct security strategy. ... With the unfortunate climate that exists in certain parts of the world, every potential risk must be considered and, preemptively, we must adapt and take measures to mitigate any risk to the event and its participants (spectators, athletes, staff, etc.).

The goal in any spectator or sports event is to ensure that the focus always remains on the participants (athletes) and the fans, and to avoid mixing in any political or social agendas, especially when these events are international and multicultural; ultimately, the goal must be to use sporting events as a platform to bring the world closer together and to help us embrace the differences that makes us unique.

YKN: *Are sporting federations, like FIFA, actively engaged in promoting sports diplomacy? And if so, can you provide any examples?*

JLF: This is not a new concept or approach—many sporting events and sporting federations have used diplomacy for both good and bad; we must not forget that throughout history, major sporting events like the Olympics, FIFA World Cups, and many others may have been used by local governments to push or promote local agendas, sometimes not necessarily in a good way.

Many events have used the platform of a major sporting event to try to "wash" many negative actions done on a local scale; we have seen many non-democratic countries, and their leaders, try to use sporting events to save face or promote a clean image when it is contrary to what they have done locally. However, we've also seen many countries and their leadership use that exact same exposure and platform to tackle many of the misconceptions that exist [about these countries].

For example, the most recent FIFA World Cup Qatar 2022 is a great example of how sports diplomacy should be used to provide objective information and depict a real image of a host nation or region.

It is no secret that prior to the FIFA World Cup in 2022, Qatar was somewhat unknown to many parts of the world [and often confused with] their neighbor Dubai, [as well as thought to be involved] with many of the conflicts prevailing in the region. What Qatar as a country did is a perfect example of what every other country hosting international sporting events should be doing, and that is to remove any preconceptions, any misinformation, and, through diplomacy, promote the reality of the country with all the positives. Qatar, as a relatively new nation, has never hidden many of the local issues they are working on to improve, but what they also did is provide a clear view to the world of the reality of the country, their people, the endless opportunities, the advantageous business ecosystem, and many more positive features. This was and is still being achieved through diplomacy and using the platform of sporting events.

One of the objectives of any nation hosting a major event is to create a legacy for the country and their people that can last into the future; surely the event will draw attention for several weeks, but it is ultimately how well a country uses the event to leave a long-lasting impression that will be a real factor of change. This could be from generating business opportunities, to promoting tourism, to promoting peace and "togetherness" through the magic of sports in an international arena.

YKN: *How can sporting events be made more inclusive of underrepresented countries, ensuring that they have equal opportunities to participate and showcase their talents on the global stage?*

JLF: It's essential to address both the logistical and structural challenges these nations face. One key strategy is to provide more-accessible qualification pathways, ensuring that teams from these regions have a fair shot at reaching global competitions. This could mean increasing the number of qualifying spots or introducing regional tournaments that give these countries more opportunities to participate.

Financial support is another critical area. Many underrepresented countries simply lack the resources to compete on an international level. By offering financial aid for travel, training, and equipment, event organizers can help level the playing field. Additionally, partnerships with local governments and organizations can help develop infrastructure and training programs that build long-term capacity.

Promotion and visibility are also crucial. Highlighting athletes and teams from underrepresented countries not only raises awareness but also inspires the next generation of talent. Media coverage, storytelling, and celebrating their achievements can highlight the narrative and show that talent exists everywhere, not just in traditional powerhouses.

Finally, fostering inclusivity means collaborating with a wide range of stakeholders, from international federations to local communities. It's about creating a global sporting community in which every country, regardless of size or resources, has the opportunity to participate and succeed. By addressing these challenges holistically, we can ensure that sporting events truly reflect the diversity and talent of the entire world.

Chapter Ten

The Cricket Matches That Served as Icebreakers

It's not often that leaders of India and Pakistan get together for any reason and they often find that cricket is the one language they both understand.

—Osman Samiuddin, author of *The Unquiet Ones: A History of Pakistan Cricket*[169]

Cricket, often dubbed a gentleman's game, has played an unexpected role in the difficult relationship between India and Pakistan. Cricket diplomacy between the two nations has long been regarded as a double-edged sword, frequently serving as a diplomatic and political instrument to bridge relations but with the cricket matches often feeling like intense battlegrounds. The rivalry between these two cricket-loving nations carries profound political and diplomatic implications, often serving as both a catalyst for tension and a platform for reconciliation.

INDIA AND PAKISTAN

The conflict between India and Pakistan is one of the modern world's most long-lasting and complex international disputes, spanning over seven decades since the partition of British India in 1947. Rooted in historical, political, and religious factors, this conflict has seen multiple wars, ongoing skirmishes, and numerous attempts at peace.

The British East India Company began its rule over the Indian subcontinent in the mid-eighteenth century, later transitioning to direct British governance following the Indian Rebellion of 1857. British India was characterized by its complex mix of religious, ethnic, and cultural groups. As British colonial rule ended, the Mountbatten Plan was implemented, leading to the partition of British India into two independent dominions, India and Pakistan, based on religious majorities. India was predominantly Hindu, while Pakistan was created as a Muslim-majority nation. The partition led to one of the largest mass migrations in history, with over ten million people crossing borders to join their respective religious majorities. This period was marked by significant communal violence, resulting in the deaths of hundreds of thousands of people.[170]

After independence, several princely states were given the choice to join either India or Pakistan. The princely state of Jammu and Kashmir, with a Hindu ruler and a Muslim-majority population, became a flashpoint. Both India and Pakistan claimed the territory, igniting the first war between the two nations in 1947. Pakistan's support for tribal militias invading Kashmir led the Maharaja of Kashmir to accede to India, prompting Indian military intervention. The war ended with a ceasefire mediated by the United Nations in 1948, resulting in a de facto border known as the Line of Control (LoC).[171]

The Cold War further complicated the situation. India, embracing a socialist path, aligned itself with the Soviet Union, while Pakistan became a U.S. ally. This fueled an arms race and a series of proxy wars within Kashmir and Afghanistan. The Indo-Pakistani War of 1965 and the Bangladesh Liberation War of 1971 were stark reminders of this period's volatility. In 1965, Pakistan initiated Operation Gibraltar, attempting to incite insurgency in Indian-administered Kashmir. This led to a full-scale war. The conflict saw intense battles, including significant tank battles in Punjab. Both nations suffered substantial losses, and the war ended with the Tashkent Agreement, mediated by the Soviet Union, leading to a return to the pre-war territorial status quo.[172]

Meanwhile, the 1970 general elections in Pakistan saw the Awami League, led by Sheikh Mujibur Rahman, win a landslide victory in the province of East Pakistan. The refusal of the Pakistani government to recognize this electoral outcome led to widespread civil disobedience and a military crackdown. India intervened in December 1971, supporting the Mukti Bahini, which were Bangladeshi guerrilla forces fighting for Rahman's political victory and the independence movement of the Bengali-speaking populations of East Pakistan (now Bangladesh). The war resulted in a decisive Indian victory, leading to the creation of the independent nation of Bangladesh. Later, in 1984, the strategic Siachen

Glacier, located in the Karakoram range, became a flashpoint when India launched Operation Meghdoot to capture key passes.[173] The region remains one of the highest and most inhospitable battlegrounds in the world, with ongoing military presence from both sides.[174]

In May 1998, India conducted a series of nuclear tests, declaring itself a nuclear-armed state. This move was met with international condemnation and sanctions. In response, Pakistan conducted its own nuclear tests in Chagai, Baluchistan, a few weeks later, establishing a nuclear deterrent against India. In early 1999, Pakistani soldiers and militants infiltrated the Kargil district of Indian-administered Kashmir, occupying strategic positions. In response, the Indian military launched Operation Vijay to evict the intruders.[175] The conflict lasted from May to July 1999, with significant casualties on both sides. International pressure, particularly from the United States, played a role in de-escalation.[176]

Cross-border terrorism has been another major factor in the ongoing conflict. Pakistan has been accused of supporting militant groups operating in Kashmir, while India has faced its own internal insurgency issues. The Agra Summit in 2001, between Indian Prime Minister Atal Bihari Vajpayee and Pakistani President Pervez Musharraf, aimed at resolving the Kashmir issue but ended without a concrete agreement. The Composite Dialogue process, initiated in 2004, covered various issues, including Kashmir, terrorism, and trade. It led to some confidence-building measures, such as opening bus routes across the Line of Control, but the dialogue process was eventually derailed by the 2008 Mumbai attacks, carried out by the Pakistan-based militant group

Lashkar-e-Taiba, resulting in over 160 deaths.[177] Following a terrorist attack on an Indian Army camp in Uri, Jammu and Kashmir, India conducted surgical strikes across the Line of Control targeting militant launchpads.[178] A suicide bombing in Pulwama, killing 40 Indian paramilitary personnel, led to Indian airstrikes on a purported terrorist training camp in Balakot, Pakistan. This escalated into aerial skirmishes, with both sides claiming to down each other's aircraft.[179] In August 2019, India revoked the special status of Jammu and Kashmir by abrogating Article 370 of its constitution, which was authorized in 1949 and stated that the two regions could have a separate constitution and state flag. This move was met with strong opposition from Pakistan, leading to increased tensions and international scrutiny. In December 2023, India's Supreme Court upheld the decision to revoke Kashmir's special status and asked the federal government to hold elections in the region by September 2024.[180]

The India-Pakistan conflict has had a devastating human cost. Thousands of soldiers and civilians have lost their lives. The ongoing violence has also slowed economic development and negatively impacted regional stability. Despite periodic efforts at dialogue, deep-seated mistrust and recurring incidents of cross-border terrorism and military skirmishes continue to hinder lasting peace. Initiatives such as trade relations, cultural exchanges, and sports diplomacy have shown potential in improving relations, but they require sustained political will and mutual trust. Moving forward, achieving lasting peace will require addressing core issues such as Kashmir and combating cross-border terrorism, which requires sustained people-to-people contact and cooperation.

CRICKET DIPLOMACY

Against these many decades of animosity, cricket has emerged as a unifying force, capturing people's imaginations on both sides of the border. The inaugural India-Pakistan cricket series in 1954 marked the beginning of reciprocal fan exchanges, creating a sense of camaraderie. However, the concept of cricket diplomacy took time to gain traction. Between 1947 and 1965, cricket engagements between India and Pakistan were limited, with only three Test series played due to geopolitical issues. Following a seventeen-year hiatus due to the aftermath of the 1965 and 1971 wars, the resumption of cricket exchanges between India and Pakistan occurred in 1978, driven by efforts from the governments led by Morarji Desai in India and Gen. Muhammad Zia-ul-Haq in Pakistan. This marked a significant turning point. The revival of cricketing ties represented the efforts of both governments to thaw frozen diplomatic relations. However, the example of Pakistani Captain Mushtaq Mohammad's speech following one of Pakistan's victories, in which he emphasized religious division, showcased the underlying tensions. Still, the cricket field became a stage for political overtures, with matches often laden with symbolic gestures of goodwill. For example, during the 2011 Cricket World Cup semi-final, the Indian Prime Minister Manmohan Singh and his Pakistani counterpart Yousuf Raza Gilani greeted and watched the match together. Both sides are also known to ease their tough visa regulations for each other during cricket matches so that thousands of fans can travel across the border.[181]

Former Pakistani President General Zia-ul-Haq initiated the "cricket for peace" concept, adding a new dimension to diplomatic discourse. One instance of cricket diplomacy occurred in February 1987, when Zia-ul-Haq attended a test match in India. Even with heightened tensions, the trip led to a meeting between Zia and the Indian Prime Minister Rajiv Gandhi, in which Zia's quiet revelation about Pakistan's nuclear capabilities served as a subtle yet significant diplomatic gesture, highlighting its sincerity and hinting at the potential for dialogue even amidst geopolitical challenges.[182]

The late Prime Minister of India, Atal Behari Vajpayee, was a staunch advocate for peace between India and Pakistan, leaving no stone unturned in his pursuit of promoting goodwill, including engaging with Pakistani President Pervez Musharraf and extending an olive branch through cricket. Vajpayee's gesture of gifting a cricket bat inscribed with the message "Win not just the game but also hearts, best wishes" to the Indian cricket team before their trip to Pakistan in 2004 exemplified his commitment to using a shared love of cricket in cultivating peace.[183]

Throughout the decades, cricket diplomacy has witnessed ups and downs, mirroring the fluctuation in the bilateral relations between the two countries. Despite India's 1989 military operations in Pakistan due to the Kashmir issue, cricket continued to be played at neutral venues like Sharjah in the United Arab Emirates. The 1990s, marked by the insurgency in Kashmir, saw cricket matches become focal points for political fervor, with fans from both nations passionately rallying behind their teams.

The early 2000s ushered in a period of cautious optimism, with cricket diplomacy reaching new heights from 2004 to 2008. It was characterized by Vajpayee's historic visit to Pakistan for the SAARC summit in 2004, a conference during which South Asian countries come together to discuss policies and relations. [184] The subsequent resumption of full-fledged cricket tours between the two countries was hailed as a symbol of newfound friendship, with cricket serving as a conduit for people-to-people diplomacy. Yet, this period of detente was short-lived, marred by the tragic events of the 2008 Mumbai attacks (also referred to as the 26/11 attacks), which cast a long shadow over bilateral relations. Recent attempts at improving diplomacy, including Prime Minister Narendra Modi's impromptu visit to Lahore in 2015, have faced challenges amid the shaky relationship.[185] While the prospect of a breakthrough in relations through cricket remains uncertain, the desire to resume cricketing ties persists among fans and officials alike.

In the years since, cricket diplomacy has continued to be a delicate balancing act, one contingent on the complexities of public sentiment. Despite its ups and downs, cricket diplomacy remains an essential force for engagement between India and Pakistan. For nearly seven decades, the scheduling and canceling of matches have served as a barometer of political relations. The future of South Asia depends on the ability of these two nuclear-armed neighbors to find a path toward coexistence and peace.

CHAPTER ELEVEN

THE LEAGUE THAT IGNITED A GLOBAL PASSION

We take these basketball programs all around the world ...
because there is this sense that we're coming in peace, that these
are universal values, that through a sport like basketball ...
[we're] teaching values that every country seems to care about—
that is teamwork, respect, hard work, etc.

—Adam Silver, NBA Commissioner[186]

THE NBA AND CHINA

With the National Basketball Association (NBA) being broadcast in over 214 countries and in more than 50 languages, basketball stands out uniquely as a global yet distinctly American sport.[187] Specifically, the NBA's presence in China has flourished in recent years, fueled by a rich history of basketball appreciation in that country dating back to the late nineteenth century. According to the NBA, basketball was introduced to China by a government official named Piengiane in 1896 after he saw Dr. James Naismith nail up a peach basket at a gymnasium in Springfield, Massachusetts.[188] Despite periods of political upheaval, including the Chinese Civil War and the Cultural Revolution, basketball persevered as a cherished pastime in China. It was endorsed by prominent leaders like Prime Minister Zhou Enlai, who orchestrated Ping-Pong Diplomacy (see part one), for its emphasis on fitness and teamwork. Following the success of Ping-Pong Diplomacy in the 1970s, both China and the United States saw sports as a valuable tool for intercultural communication.

The 1979 visit by the Washington Bullets (now Wizards) to China was a landmark moment. It marked the beginning of a long and fascinating relationship between the NBA and China. Two exhibition games against the Chinese national team and the "Bayi" army team laid the foundation for a lasting connection between the two countries.[189] Capitalizing on a growing interest in the sport, David Stern, the visionary NBA commissioner, made a pivotal move in 1987. He secured a deal with CCTV, China's state-controlled television network, to broadcast NBA Finals games.[190] This deal was the official entry of the NBA into China, with the sport surpassing table tennis as the primary vehicle for sports diplomacy between the United States and China.

Later, in 2002, the arrival of native son Yao Ming to the NBA—specifically the Houston Rockets—changed basketball in China, with Ming igniting a genuine enthusiasm for the sport with his talent and charisma. As the first overall pick in the NBA draft, Ming became a symbol of unity and pride for both nations. Millions tuned in to watch him play, making him an overnight global ambassador for the sport. Standing at 7'6", Ming was a towering figure both on and off the court, and his tenure with the Rockets propelled basketball to new heights of popularity among the younger generations in China.[191] NBA teams began scouting China for the next potential star, and the league actively pursued expansion into this vast market. In 2021, Tencent, China's internet giant, secured broadcasting rights to the NBA, making hundreds of games accessible to the fans. The NBA cultivated its presence further through social media initiatives and strategic partnerships with teams like the Houston Rockets, who are now forever linked to Yao.

The NBA's investment in China has yielded significant returns, with broadcast revenue, sponsorship deals, and merchandise sales driving exponential growth in the market. Tencent's streaming services have enabled millions of Chinese fans to access NBA content, while sponsorship agreements with leading brands have further solidified the league's profitable business in the country. Additionally, pre-season games held in China have consistently sold out within minutes.[192] According to the NBA, in 2009, "89 percent of Chinese people ages 15 to 5 [were] more aware of the NBA than of the World Table Tennis Championships, the European Champions League, and even the FIFA World Cup."[193] Moreover, the NBA's influence extends beyond sports, shaping popular culture and social media trends in China. NBA stars like Kobe Bryant, Stephen Curry, and LeBron James enjoy widespread recognition and adoration, with millions of Chinese fans following their every move online. Bryant's untimely passing in 2020 sparked an outpouring of grief and tributes across China, a reminder of the profound impact of basketball on the nation's collective consciousness.[194]

The NBA's journey in China is a story of mutual benefit. Over the years, the NBA's relationship with China has evolved into a dynamic partnership encompassing economic collaboration and mutual respect. The inherent appeal of basketball, with its emphasis on teamwork, skill, and athleticism, resonates deeply with Chinese audiences. They admire the craft and finesse of guards and wings—players who excel despite not being the biggest on the court. This passion is the foundation upon which the NBA has built a remarkable presence in China. As the NBA continues to expand its global footprint, China remains a cornerstone of its international growth strategy. From the early days of basketball diplomacy to the present era of digital media and global marketing, the NBA has played a central role in shaping the cultural landscape of China, fueled by a shared love for the game of basketball.

BASKETBALL GOODWILL TOUR TO NORTH KOREA

In the case of North Korea, a country shrouded in secrecy, basketball diplomacy has emerged as an unexpected and powerful tool for engagement. North Korea's relationship with the outside world has long been characterized by tension, suspicion, and isolation. The regime's authoritarian rule and nuclear ambitions have perpetuated a sense of enigma and intrigue on the global stage. But basketball holds a special place in North Korean society, with the sport enjoying popularity among both elites and ordinary citizens. The regime's leader, Kim Jong-un, has a fascination for basketball, which might be the only thing that the North Korean supreme leader likes about the United States.

Recognizing the potential of sports diplomacy to foster communication and understanding, the media company VICE took on a groundbreaking initiative in 2013: basketball diplomacy in North Korea. Leveraging the shared passion for basketball, the documentary team orchestrated a goodwill game featuring iconic figures such as the Harlem Globetrotters and North Korea's national team. This unprecedented exchange between athletes served as a catalyst for dialogue and cooperation, defying conventional notions of diplomacy. The journey into North Korea presented numerous challenges, including strict government oversight and surveillance, as well as state propaganda. The documentary team navigated a labyrinth of restrictions and protocols, facing constant scrutiny from minders and officials. However, amidst these obstacles, moments of genuine connection and empathy emerged. The culmination of the documentary, featuring a surreal encounter with Kim Jong-un himself, underscored the goal of the trip in using basketball diplomacy to better understand North Korea. While acknowledging the limitations of such initiatives in effecting systemic change, the documentary highlighted the importance of dialogue, understanding, and empathy. By humanizing the people of North Korea and challenging stereotypes, basketball diplomacy offered a chance for the U.S. to establish a relationship amidst geopolitical tensions.[195]

Famously, the five-time NBA champion Dennis Rodman was the star of the basketball trip to North Korea. The world watched with a mix of curiosity and incredulity as the former

NBA star visited Pyongyang to watch an exhibition basketball game featuring the Harlem Globetrotters alongside Kim Jong-un, a self-professed fan of the 1990s Chicago Bulls, for whom Rodman played three seasons. What ensued was a series of events that blurred the lines between sports, diplomacy, and personal relationships, leaving a lasting impact on both Rodman's legacy and the geopolitics of the Korean Peninsula.

Rodman's initial interactions with Kim Jong-un were marked by an unexpected camaraderie, with Rodman in subsequent interviews declaring the dictator his "friend for life" and a "great guy." He even went as far as to suggest that then-President Barack Obama call Kim on the telephone and publicly asked Kim to do him "a solid" and release Kenneth Bae, a Korean-American Christian missionary who'd been detained in North Korea since 2012. Rodman's public plea for Kim to "cut Kenneth Bae loose" pointed to the complexities of his role as an unofficial envoy, in which he oscillated between establishing personal connections and foregrounding international humanitarian concerns. Undeterred in his mission to bridge the gap between North Korea and the United States through basketball, Rodman went on subsequent visits to Pyongyang, emphasizing his goal to train North Korean players and establish a basketball league in the isolated nation. Rodman's involvement in North Korean affairs took on a new dimension with the inauguration of President Trump, as he presented Trump's business book *The Art of the Deal* to North Korean Sports Minister Kim Il Guk during a visit to Pyongyang. Despite assertions from the Trump Administration that Rodman had no official diplomatic role, his presence in North Korea during the historic Singapore Summit between Trump and Kim Jong-un was a clear indicator of his enduring influence on diplomatic discourse between the two nuclear powers.[196]

During the basketball goodwill trip, there were moments that showed clear human connection, such as a simple lunch during which players from vastly different backgrounds converged. Despite language barriers, the language of sports facilitated communication, shedding light on the athletes' shared experiences and aspirations irrespective of nationality. The North Korean players, though initially reserved, opened up about their recent game with the Harlem Globetrotters. Their accounts revealed a mix of nerves and excitement, due to the universal emotions accompanying athletic competition. As they reminisced about particular moments on the court, a North Korean "Marshall" unexpectedly joined the gathering. Yet, even these constraints did not prevent opportunities for meaningful engagement.

While the basketball trip and Rodman's actions have sparked controversy and debate, they have also shed light on the potential of unconventional diplomacy to make way for dialogue that might not be possible otherwise. Through genuine engagement and mutual respect, athletes become ambassadors of goodwill. Moreover, the significance of this exchange has extended beyond the immediate participants, resonating with audiences worldwide. Sports diplomacy challenges stereotypes, encourages empathy, and inspires hope for a future built on dialogue and collaboration rather than discord.

CHAPTER TWELVE

A DIFFERENT KIND OF
SPORTS DIPLOMACY

*To say that politics is not a part of sports is not being realistic.
When I run, I am more than a runner. I am a diplomat, an
ambassador for my country.*

—Filbert Bayi, Tanzanian athlete, former 1500m world
record holder[197]

While the events described in this chapter may not fit
the traditional mold of sports diplomacy involving direct
diplomatic engagement, they can still be considered forms
of sports diplomacy because of their significant symbolic,
cultural, and ideological impact. They have helped shape
global perceptions, showcase national values, and contribute
to the broader context of international relations by influencing

how nations and peoples view each other.

JESSE OWENS AT THE 1936 BERLIN OLYMPICS

The 1936 Summer Olympics, held in Berlin, Germany, were intended by Adolf Hitler and the Nazi regime to showcase the superiority of the Aryan race and the might of the Third Reich. The games were meticulously organized to impress the international community and to project an image of a powerful and united Germany. The Nazis invested heavily in infrastructure, including the construction of the massive Olympic Stadium, and ensured that the event would be a grand spectacle. However, the games took an unexpected turn with the remarkable performance of African-American athletes. They showed the world that racism has no place in sports and that all athletes, regardless of their background, should be judged on their abilities and merits. These athletes, including Jesse Owens, Ralph Metcalfe, and John Woodruff, won a total of fourteen medals in various events. It was a massive blow to the Nazi party's beliefs, as they had previously claimed that Black people were inferior to the Aryan race. Jesse Owens, in particular, had a significant impact on the Games: he won four gold medals, in the 100-meter dash, 200-meter dash, long jump, and 4x100-meter relay. Owens's victories were even more remarkable given the discrimination he faced as a Black athlete in America. He persevered to go on to become one of the most celebrated and influential Olympic athletes of all time.[198]

During the 1930s, African Americans in the United States faced severe racial segregation and discrimination. Jim Crow laws in the South enforced racial segregation, while de facto discrimination existed in the North. Jesse Owens was born in Alabama and grew up in Cleveland, Ohio. Despite the challenges posed by racial discrimination, he excelled in athletics, breaking several records during his high school and college years. In Berlin, Owens won his first gold medal in the 100 meters and his second gold in the long jump, where he set an Olympic record. A memorable moment of sportsmanship occurred when the German competitor Luz Long, who finished second, gave Owens advice on his technique. Owens secured his third gold in the 200 meters, and the final gold came as part of the 4x100 meter relay team, where Owens and his teammates set a world record.[199]

Owens's success as an African-American athlete was a powerful counterpoint to the German regime's racist ideologies. Owens's achievements garnered significant international attention and helped to enhance the United States' international image of the United States by showcasing the country's potential for diversity and inclusion despite its internal racial struggles. The friendship and sportsmanship displayed Luz Long, who congratulated Owens and walked arm-in-arm with him, further provided a poignant moment of shared humanity amidst such a differing of ideologies across the world. The moment was captured by the film director Leni Riefenstahl, whose job, ironically, was to showcase Germany's superior abilities.[200]

BLOOD IN THE WATER

The 1956 water polo match between the Soviet Union and Hungary at the Melbourne Olympics is one of the most storied and emotionally charged events in sports history. Known as the "Blood in the Water" match, it was a symbol of national pride for Hungary.

After World War II, Hungary fell within the Soviet sphere of influence, becoming a satellite state of the Soviet Union. The imposition of a communist regime led to widespread dissatisfaction among Hungarians, who longed for greater political freedom and national sovereignty. In October 1956, a spontaneous nationwide revolt broke out against the Soviet-imposed policies. The uprising, fueled by demands for political reform and national independence, saw students, workers, and soldiers unite in protest against the oppressive regime. Initially, the Soviets seemed willing to negotiate, but they soon launched a brutal military intervention to crush the rebellion. By early November, the uprising was brutally suppressed, resulting in thousands of Hungarian casualties and a wave of refugees fleeing to the West.[201]

Despite the turmoil at home, the Hungarian water polo team traveled to Melbourne to compete in the 1956 Olympics. The team was among the best in the world, having won gold in the 1952 Helsinki Olympics. The Soviet team was also a strong contender, setting the stage for a high-stakes confrontation in the water. The match between Hungary and the Soviet Union took place against the recent turmoil of the Hungarian Revolution; for the Hungarian players, it was an opportunity to assert their national dignity and protest Soviet oppression.

The semi-final match was held on December 6. The match was fiercely contested, characterized by aggressive play, violent altercations, and physical confrontations. The most iconic moment of the match occurred when the Hungarian player Ervin Zador was struck by a Soviet player, resulting in a gash over his eye. The pool turned red with blood, and the match descended into chaos, with the crowd reacting vehemently against the Soviet team. Nonetheless, Hungary emerged victorious, with a 4-0 win. The victory was celebrated not only as a sporting achievement but also as a triumph over Soviet oppression. It represented a moment of moral victory for the Hungarian people, who had suffered greatly during the uprising and its suppression. The players were hailed as heroes, embodying the national spirit and resistance against foreign control. The image of Zador with blood streaming down his face became an enduring symbol of Hungary's struggle for freedom. At the awards ceremony, Zador was laughing and crying at the same time. He was crying for Hungary because he knew he would not have a home to return to.[202]

The Blood in the Water match is remembered as one of the most dramatic and significant events in Olympic history. The match is commemorated in Hungary as a poignant reminder of the 1956 Revolution and the desire for national sovereignty and human rights. It remains a source of inspiration for future generations. The match drew international attention to the plight of Hungary under Soviet rule, garnering sympathy and support from around the world. It helped to expose the brutal reality of life under communist regimes and the lengths to which people would go to assert their independence.

RUMBLE IN THE JUNGLE

The "Rumble in the Jungle" was a historic boxing match held on October 30, 1974, in Kinshasa, Zaire (now the Democratic Republic of the Congo). The fight featured

Muhammad Ali, the former heavyweight champion, against the then reigning champion, George Foreman. The event is remembered for Ali's dramatic victory and its significant cultural and political implications. Mobutu Sese Seko, the president of Zaire, saw the fight as an opportunity to promote his country on the global stage and legitimize his regime—he aimed to showcase Zaire's independence and potential as a modern African nation by hosting the event. The event was set against a continent emerging from the shadows of colonialism. Many African nations were seeking to establish their identities and assert their place in the world.

Ali was not just a boxer; he was a prominent figure in the civil rights movement and a vocal critic of the Vietnam War. His refusal to be drafted and his subsequent legal battles made him a symbol of resistance and resilience. After Ali had been stripped of his titles and banned from boxing for several years, his return to the ring was more than a comeback—it was a fight for redemption and reaffirmation of his beliefs and identity. George Foreman was a fearsome opponent known for his formidable punching power. Many considered him unbeatable, making Ali the underdog. Ali's strategy, known as the "rope-a-dope," involved leaning against the ropes, allowing Foreman to throw punches that gradually exhausted him. In the eighth round, Ali launched a series of precise punches, knocking Foreman out and reclaiming the heavyweight title.[203]

The fight was watched by an estimated one billion viewers worldwide, making it one of the most-watched televised events in history. Ali's connection with Africa, his embrace of African culture, and his status as a global icon of Black pride resonated deeply with many Africans and the African diaspora.[204] His victory was celebrated as a symbolic victory for the oppressed and marginalized. By hosting the fight, Mobutu showcased Zaire's cultural heritage, traditions, and modern aspirations to a global audience, as well as promoted a sense of national pride and unity among Zaireans. The Rumble in the Jungle continues to resonate as a symbol of African empowerment and the potential for sports to drive positive change on the continent.

MIRACLE ON ICE

The "Miracle on Ice" refers to the ice hockey game during the 1980 Winter Olympics in Lake Placid, New York, in which the amateur team from the United States triumphed over the heavily favored Soviet Union. This event is widely regarded as an ideological victory for the United States in the context of the Cold War. (As you'll recall, after World War II, the United States and the Soviet Union emerged as the two global superpowers, leading to a protracted period of geopolitical tension known as the Cold War. This era was marked by ideological conflicts, military confrontations, and a race for technological and cultural superiority.)

By the 1980s, the Soviet Union had established itself as a dominant force in international ice hockey, winning numerous World Championships and Olympic gold medals. The Soviet team was composed of seasoned professionals who were essentially full-time athletes. The United States, meanwhile, was emerging from significant challenges in the late 1970s, including economic stagflation, the energy crisis, the aftermath of the Vietnam War, and the Iranian hostage crisis.[205] In stark contrast to the Soviet team, the U.S. Olympic hockey team was made up of amateur and collegiate players, many of whom were under the age of twenty-one, a disparity in experience that highlighted the David-versus-Goliath nature of the matchup. The U.S. team was coached by Herb Brooks, a former Olympian with a rigorous and innovative approach to training. Brooks emphasized conditioning, teamwork, and a strategic style of play that blended European finesse with North American physicality. Brooks selected players based on their compatibility with his vision, favoring speed, agility, and a willingness to embrace his demanding regimen. The team underwent extensive training and exhibition matches to prepare for the Olympics.

The U.S. team entered the Games with modest expectations but quickly gained momentum. They tied with Sweden and defeated strong teams like Czechoslovakia, Norway, Romania, and West Germany to advance to the medal round. The Soviet Union, having dominated their group, advanced to face the United States.[206]

The game began with the Soviets taking an early lead, but the U.S. team managed to keep pace. A critical moment came when Mark Johnson scored with one second remaining in the first period, tying the game 2-2. The Soviets regained the lead, but the U.S. goaltender Jim Craig made numerous key saves to keep the game within reach. In a stunning turn of events, the U.S. team scored two quick goals, with Mike Eruzione's game-winning goal putting them ahead 4-3. The U.S. defense and Craig's goaltending had withstood the Soviet onslaught in the final minutes, securing the improbable victory.[207]

The victory was celebrated across the United States, with

Americans viewing it as a triumph of the underdog and a testament to the nation's resilience and spirit. The game was broadcast on tape delay, with the broadcaster Al Michaels's famous call, "Do you believe in miracles? Yes!" becoming an iconic moment in sports broadcasting history.[208] The victory was seen as a vindication of American values such as freedom, democracy, and individualism. The amateur status of the U.S. players highlighted the contrast between the free society that nurtured them and the regimented, state-controlled system of the Soviet Union.

At a time when the United States was grappling with self-doubt and a perceived decline in global standing, the Miracle on Ice provided a symbolic boost. It reinforced the belief that the American way of life, despite its flaws, could prevail against the disciplined and authoritarian model of the Soviet Union. The game underscored the cultural and ideological battle lines of the Cold War. It became a metaphor for the larger struggle between the two superpowers, offering Americans a moment of national unity and pride. While the game did not directly influence Cold War policies, it contributed to the larger narrative of American resilience and eventual triumph. It was a precursor to the more assertive stance the United States would adopt in the 1980s under President Ronald Reagan, who emphasized the need to challenge Soviet influence globally.

The Miracle on Ice remains one of the most celebrated moments in American sports history. It has been immortalized in films, documentaries, and books, and continues to inspire generations of athletes and fans. The story is often used as an educational tool to teach lessons about perseverance, teamwork, and the broader context of the Cold War. In times of national difficulty, the Miracle on Ice reminds us that the human spirit still triumphs against all daunting odds.

THE HAND OF GOD GOAL

The 1986 FIFA World Cup quarter-final match between Argentina and England is one of the most memorable and controversial matches in the history of soccer. Played on June 22, 1986, in Mexico City, the match featured two iconic goals scored by the Argentine legend Diego Maradona: the "Hand of God" and the "Goal of the Century." These goals secured Argentina a hugely controversial victory.

In 1982, Argentina and the United Kingdom had engaged in a brief but intense conflict over the Falkland Islands, which lie off the coast of South America and are known in Argentina as the Islas Malvinas. The war resulted in a decisive British victory but left deep scars and lingering animosities between the two nations. For Argentina, the defeat was a source of national trauma; the 1986 World Cup provided an opportunity for redemption on the international stage.[209]

By 1986, Diego Maradona was already considered one of the greatest footballers in the world, known for his skill, vision, and creativity on the field. For many Argentinians, Maradona symbolized hope and resilience—his playing in the World Cup was seen as a chance to restore national pride. The match between Argentina and England was a highly anticipated quarter-final clash, drawing significant attention due to both sides' political history and athletic talent.

In the fifty-first minute, Maradona scored the infamous "Hand of God" goal. As he leaped to challenge English goalkeeper Peter Shilton for the ball, Maradona used his left hand to punch the ball into the net. Despite protests from the English players, the goal was allowed to stand. Just four minutes later, Maradona scored what would later be called the "Goal of the Century." He dribbled from his own half, evading three English defenders and the goalkeeper to score a brilliant solo goal. This goal showcased Maradona's extraordinary talent and was voted "the goal of the [twentieth] century" in a 2002 FIFA poll.[210]

For Argentina, the victory over England was seen as a form of poetic justice and national vindication. It allowed Argentinians to reclaim a sense of pride and identity tarnished by the defeat in the Falklands War. Maradona's performance elevated him to the status of a national hero. His actions on the field resonated deeply with the Argentine people, who viewed the victory as a triumph over their former adversaries.

The "Hand of God" goal challenged the conventions of fairness and sportsmanship, highlighting the complex relationship between morality and competition in sports. Maradona's candid admission later that it was scored "a little with the head of Maradona and a little with the hand of God" added to his legendary status. The match and Maradona's goals received extensive media coverage, bringing global attention to the political and cultural tensions between Argentina and England. Despite the controversy, Maradona's brilliance was universally acknowledged, generating a sense of mutual respect and admiration across national boundaries.

USAIN BOLT'S 2008 BEIJING OLYMPICS RECORDS

Usain Bolt's performance at the 2008 Beijing Olympics is one of the most iconic moments in the history of sports. Bolt, a Jamaican sprinter, captivated the world with his extraordinary speed and charismatic personality. On August 16, 2008, Bolt won the 100-meter final with a time of 9.69 seconds, breaking the world record. His performance was remarkable not only for its speed but also for the ease with which he achieved it, celebrating before crossing the finish line. Four days later, Bolt won the 200-meter final in 19.30 seconds, breaking Michael Johnson's 12-year-old world record. This victory made him the first man to break both the 100-meter and 200-meter world records at the same Olympics. Bolt's achievements in Beijing solidified his status as the fastest man in the world.[211]

Bolt's charisma and joyful celebration made him a beloved figure worldwide, promoting a positive image of sportsmanship; his achievements and his journey to the top inspired countless young athletes around the world. Bolt's global fame also attracted tourism to and investment in Jamaica and contributed to cultural diplomacy by showcasing the country's vibrant culture, music, and athletic talent. Visitors were drawn to the island nation to experience its rich cultural heritage and to connect with the home of the world's fastest man, whose performances were celebrated as expressions of Jamaican identity and creativity.

Bolt's records and achievements at the 2008 Beijing Olympics remain benchmarks in the history of athletics. His impact extends beyond sport, however, as he remains a cultural icon and an ambassador for Jamaica. His influence is evident in various aspects of popular culture, from music and fashion to advertising and philanthropy. Now, the Usain Bolt Foundation is creating opportunities through education in Jamaica by providing school materials. These days, Bolt is also focused on mitigating the effects of climate change in the Caribbean.

Global Initiatives

People are not listening to the same news; they are not communicating on the same wavelength. We need to break down those barriers: sports and cultural exchanges—human connections start there. If you can communicate person to person, it rises up the chain ... to make our leaders able to make those kinds of changes.

—Judy Hoarfrost, U.S. national table tennis player who visited China in 1971[212]

On the relationship between sports and politics, Sarah Hirshland, CEO of the U.S. Olympic and Paralympic Committee, comments, "Our country is the leader in sports around the world and the influence we have is palpable everywhere you go. So, are politics and sports inextricably linked? In ways, yes. But can sports transcend and rise above politics? I'd like to believe the answer to that is yes."[213] Across the modern era, sports diplomacy has emerged as a powerful yet underutilized tool in international relations, through its promotion of cultural understanding and cooperation between nations. This concluding chapter provides examples of several countries' formal efforts—as opposed to the informal or ad hoc events described in previous chapters—in sports diplomacy, highlighting notable initiatives and their impact.

United States: Sports Diplomacy Division, Bureau of Educational and Cultural Affairs

The United States has been at the forefront of sports diplomacy through initiatives led by the Bureau of Educational and Cultural Affairs (ECA). The ECA's Sports Diplomacy Division runs several programs aimed at building international relationships. The Sports Envoy Program, for example, sends current and retired professional athletes and coaches overseas to conduct clinics and workshops, engaging youth and promoting mutual understanding. The Sports Visitor Program brings non-elite athletes and coaches to the United States for a short-term sports exchange, offering participants a chance to learn about American culture and sports practices while sharing their own cultures. Since 2007, the Sports Envoy Program has sent more than 300 groups on behalf of the United States to over 130 counties, with the goal of "deliver[ing] high-impact programming and improv[ing] diplomatic relations."[214] Since 2018, the Sports Visitor Program has had over 1,000 participants, traveling to more than 80 countries.

United Kingdom: International Inspiration Programme, British Council

The United Kingdom utilizes sports diplomacy through the British Council's International Inspiration Programme, launched around the London 2012 Olympics. This program focuses on several essential principles: First is youth empowerment; the goal is to engage young people in sports to build skills and confidence. Second is community development, which uses sports to address social issues such as gender inequality and social inclusion. Third is international cooperation, or partnering with organizations worldwide to promote sports as a tool for development and peace. The International Inspiration Programme has reached over 25 million children and has trained over 250,000 practitioners.[215]

Japan: Sports for Tomorrow Programme

Japan's Sports for Tomorrow (SFT) Programme, initiated ahead of the Tokyo 2020 Summer Olympics, aims to contribute to international peace and development through sports. SFT focuses on international exchange, facilitating sports exchanges between Japanese and international athletes; educational initiatives, promoting sports education to improve health and well-being; and disaster recovery, using sports to support communities affected by natural disasters. The SFT Programme is committed to reaching over 10 million people from more than 100 countries. Some of the SFT initiatives include providing young girls in Kenya the opportunity to play table tennis and introducing a radio calisthenics routine in Malaysia that is accessible to anyone. Additionally, SFT deepens understanding of Japanese sports by hosting seminars and demonstrations of martial arts like judo, karate, aikido, and kendo worldwide. In Bosnia and Herzegovina, SFT supported the rehabilitation of the Mostar City Sports Center, promoting reconciliation among children from different ethnic groups who now enjoy sports together. Daichi Suzuki, commissioner of the Japan Sports Agency, emphasizes that Japanese sports focus on education, character building, and personal discipline, hoping SFT will help others experience this Japanese spirit.[216]

Australia: Sport for Development Programme

Australia's Sport for Development Programme, or Team Up, is led by the Australian Sports Commission. The program comprises more than thirty partnerships across the Asia-Pacific region. Team Up aims to create sports programs that attract and retain women, girls, and people with disabilities, as well as men and boys. Team Up is also ensuring that sports are safe, inclusive, and accessible. Key activities include: capacity building—training coaches and sports administrators to enhance local sports infrastructure; health promotion—using sports to promote physical activity and combat non-communicable diseases; and gender equality—encouraging female participation in sports to promote women's empowerment. Team Up's Australian and Asia-Pacific partners are using "sport to strengthen relationships and build closer collaboration."[217]

Germany: Engagement Through Sport and Integration Through Sports Programs

Germany's Engagement Through Sport Program, coordinated by the German Olympic Sports Confederation (DOSB), focuses on international cooperation, peace-building, and education. Meanwhile, the federal program Integration Through Sports, established in 1989, aims to promote self-reliance, social cohesion, and local integration for refugees and migrants in Germany.[218] By providing financial support, resources and equipment, and intercultural training to local sports clubs and associations, Integration Through Sports helps these clubs and associations offer customized services to thousands of migrants. These services use sports to empower migrants to navigate everyday life challenges, enhance their intercultural competencies, and facilitate interactions with local authorities. The program's robust political and societal support is reflected in its ample budget of 11.4 million euros, last reported in 2017, ensuring its growing influence in Germany. Challenges such as navigating cultural differences and language barriers are mitigated through strong collaborations with local migrant organizations, providing cultural knowledge and language tutoring alongside sports activities. This initiative not only boosts the self-confidence and social integration of refugees and migrants but also promotes intercultural bonds and community spirit, making sports clubs more vibrant and inclusive.[219]

When visiting China in 1984, President Ronald Reagan told Chinese college students that "friendship between people is the basis of friendship between governments."[220] Sports diplomacy is a growing field with significant contributions to establishing friendships between people in an increasingly more connected world. By leveraging the universal appeal of sports, these initiatives promote cultural understanding, peace, and development, demonstrating the decisive role of sports in international relations. As Jan Berris, vice president of the National Committee on U.S.-China Relations, so eloquently put it, "If the two governments want to put sanctions on each other and yell at each other and find faults with each other constantly, let them go do it. In the 70s ... the United States and China both began taking actions which set the stage for the growth of people-to-people exchanges, and I wish we could get back to that where both governments would step back and just let people like us keep going and engaging with one another."[221]

NOTES

1. Nelson Mandela, "Sport has the power to change the world," Laureus Lifetime Achievement Award Speech, accessed Mar. 25, 2022, https://www.laureus.com/about.

2. Andrew Strenk, "Diplomats in Track Suits: the Role of Sports in the Foreign Policy of the German Democratic Republic," *Journal of Sport and Social Issues* 4, no 1 (1980): 34-45.

3. Eleanor Albert, "The Mixed Record of Sports Diplomacy, Council on Foreign Relations," Council on Foreign Relations, last modified Feb. 6, 2018, https://www.cfr.org/interview/mixed-record-sports-diplomacy.

4. "1984 Summer Olympics," Olympedia, accessed June 22, 2023, https://www.olympedia.org/editions/21.

5. Daniel Trotta and Sarah Marsh, "Cuban deal with MLB allows players to sign without defecting," Reuters, last modified Dec. 19, 2018, https://www.reuters.com/article/sports/cuban-deal-with-mlb-allows-players-to-sign-without-defecting-idUSKC-N1OI2L5.

6. "Do Sports Belong in Diplomacy? What Leaders from the NBA, Olympics and College Think," Duke Today, last modified Sep. 29, 2023, https://today.duke.edu/2023/09/do-sports-belong-diplomacy-what-leaders-nba-olympics-and-college-think.

7. Barry Sanders, "Sport as Public Diplomacy," *Sports Diplomacy* 2, no. 6 (2011), https://uscpublicdiplomacy.org/pdin_monitor_article/sport-public-diplomacy.

8. Richard Nixon, *RN: The Memoirs of Richard Nixon* (Simon &

Schuster, 1990).

9. "41 Years Ago – The Week that Changed the World," Richard Nixon Foundation, last modified Feb. 21, 2013, https://www.nixonfoundation.org/2013/02/41-years-ago-the-week-that-changed-the-world.

10. Evan Andrews, "How Ping-Pong Diplomacy Thawed the Cold War," History, last modified Oct. 19, 2018, https://www.history.com/news/ping-pong-diplomacy.

11. Jonathan DeHart, "The Legacy of Ping-Pong Diplomat Zhuang Zedong," *The Diplomat*, Feb. 13, 2013, https://thediplomat.com/2013/02/the-legacy-of-ping-pong-diplomat-zhuang-zedong.

12. "Ping Pong Diplomacy And Secret Henry Kissinger Visits To China," Facts and Details, last modified Aug. 2021, https://factsanddetails.com/china/cat2/sub6/entry-5535.html.

13. "Ping-Pong Diplomacy: Artifacts from the Historic 1971 U.S. Table Tennis Trip to China," National Museum of American Diplomacy, last modified August 5, 2021, https://diplomacy.state.gov/ping-pong-diplomacy-historic-1971-u-s-table-tennis-trip-to-china.

14. Mayumi Itoh, *The Origin of Ping-Pong Diplomacy: The Forgotten Architect of Sino-U.S. Rapprochement* (Palgrave Macmillan, 2011).

15. Jung Chang and Jon Halliday, *Mao: The Unknown Story* (Jonathan Cape, 2005).

16. Itoh, *The Origin of Ping-Pong Diplomacy*.

17. Hongshan Li, *Fighting on the Cultural Front: U.S.-China Relations in the Cold War* (Columbia University Press, 2024).

18. Andrews, "How Ping-Pong Diplomacy."

19. "Ping Pong Diplomacy," PBS, accessed July 4, 2023, https://www.pbs.org/wgbh/americanexperience/features/china-

ping-pong.

20. "The World: The Ping Heard Round the World," *Time*, Apr. 26, 1971.

21. David Owen, "Hello China! Ping-pong diplomacy and the value of spontaneity when building bridges through sport," Inside the Games, last modified Apr. 14, 2021, https://www.insidethegames.biz/articles/1106599/ping-pong-diplomacy-china-sport.

22. "Ping-Pong Diplomacy: Artifacts."

23. "Ping-Pong Diplomacy: Artifacts."

24. Steven V. Roberts, "'Ping-pong Diplomacy: The Secret History Behind the Game That Changed the World' by Nicholas Griffin," *Washington Post*, Jan. 24, 2014, https://www.washingtonpost.com/opinions/ping-pong-diplomacy-the-secret-history-behind-the-game-that-changed-the-world-by-nicholas-griffin/2014/01/24/03e10536-794f-11e3-af7f-13bf0e9965f6_story.html.

25. "Foreign Policy: Red China and Russia," UPI, last modified 1971, https://www.upi.com/Archives/Audio/Events-of-1971/Foreign-Policy-Red-China-and-Russia.

26. "Ping-Pong Diplomacy: Artifacts."

27. Andrews, "How Ping-Pong Diplomacy."

28. Andrews, "How Ping-Pong Diplomacy."

29. Guanhua Wang, "'Friendship First': China's Sports Diplomacy during the Cold War," *The Journal of American-East Asian Relations* 12, no. 3/4 (2003): 133–53.

30. Brian Bridges, "Driver of Peace? Ping-Pong Diplomacy on The Korean Peninsula," *International Journal of Korean History* 25, No. 2 (2020): 75-102.

31. Serzh Sargsyan, "We Are Ready to Talk to Turkey," *Wall Street Journal*, July 9, 2008, https://wsj.com/articles/

SB121555668872637291.

32. Chairman Mao Zhedong. From Andrews, "How Ping-Pong Diplomacy."

33. President Richard Nixon. From "41 Years Ago." https://www.nixonfoundation.org/2013/02/41-years-ago-the-week-that-changed-the-world.

34. "Nixon Legacy Forum Transcript: The Opening to China: A Discussion with Henry Kissinger," Richard Nixon Foundation, last modified March 7, 2012, https://www.nixonfoundation.org/wp-content/uploads/2019/04/Nixon-Legacy-Forum-A-Discussion-With-Henry-Kissinger-on-The-Opening-to-China.pdf.

35. "Nixon Legacy Forum Transcript."

36. "Nixon Presidential Materials," NSC Files, Box 1319, NSC Unfiled Material, 1969, 1 of 19, White House Special Files, President's Office Files, Box 1, President's handwriting File, January 1969, National Archives, Last modified Feb. 1, 1969, https://history.state.gov/historicaldocuments/frus1969-76v17/d3.

37. More original documents on U.S.-China relations, September 1970-July 1971, can be found in "The Beijing-Washington Back-Channel and Henry Kissinger's Secret Trip to China," National Security Archive Electronic Briefing Book No. 66, ed. William Burr, The National Security Archive, last modified Feb. 27, 2002, https://nsarchive2.gwu.edu/NSAEBB/NSAEBB66.

38. Henry A. Kissinger, "My talk with Chou En-lai," USC US-China Institute, last modified July 14, 1971, https://china.usc.edu/sites/default/files/article/attachments/19710714-kissinger-to-nixon-on-secret-meetings-in-china.pdf.

39. Richard Nixon, "Remarks to the Nation Announcing Acceptance of an Invitation To Visit the People's Republic of Chi-

na," The American Presidency Project, last modified July 15, 1971, https://www.presidency.ucsb.edu/documents/remarks-the-nation-announcing-acceptance-invitation-visit-the-peoples-republic-china.

40. Michael E. Ruane, "China was a brutal communist menace. In 1972, Richard Nixon visited, anyway," *Washington Post*, Feb. 20, 2022, https://www.washingtonpost.com/history/2022/02/20/nixon-china-mao-visit-1972.

41. "Joint Communique between the United States and China." Wilson Center, last modified Feb. 28, 1972, https://digitalarchive.wilsoncenter.org/document/joint-communique-between-united-states-and-china.

42. "Nixon's China Game Timeline," PBS, accessed June 3, 2023, https://www.pbs.org/wgbh/americanexperience/features/china-timeline.

43. Nancy Bernkopf Tucker, "China as a Factor in the Collapse of the Soviet Empire," *Political Science Quarterly* 110, no. 4 (1995): 501–18.

44. "List of countries with which China has diplomatic relations," Ministry of Foreign Affairs of China, accessed June 23, 2023, https://www.mfa.gov.cn/web/ziliao_674904/2193_674977/200812/t20081221_9284708.shtml.

45. Richard Nixon, "Foundations of Foreign Policy, 1969-1972," *Foreign Affairs* 46, no. 1 (1967): 113-125.

46. Jan Berris, Judy Hoarfrost, and Doug Spelman, "Celebrating the 50th Anniversary of Ping Pong Diplomacy," hosted by the National Committee on U.S.-China Relations on Apr. 28, 2021, https://www.youtube.com/watch?v=EjAV0D5FwW8. Jan Berris accompanied the Chinese table tennis delegation in the United States in 1972.

47. Jing Zhang, "The Origins, Practices, and Narratives of Sino-American Civilian Technological Exchanges (1971-1978),"

The Chinese Journal of American Studies 5 (2020): 122-160.

48. Pete Millwood, "An 'Exceedingly Delicate Undertaking': Sino-American Science Diplomacy, 1966–78," *Journal of Contemporary History* 56, no 1 (2021): 166-190.

49. Jingjing Su and Daqing Zhang, "A study on the first medical delegation from New China to the United States," Science Spring, last modified Aug.14, 2017, https://baike.baidu.com/tashuo/browse/content?id=b05f0ad88174b62e06440318.

50. Millwood, "An 'Exceedingly Delicate Undertaking'."

51. "Cultural Exchange Bridges China and US," Xinhua News Agency, last modified Feb. 15, 2002, http://www.china.org.cn/english/2002/Feb/27044.htm.

52. Robert Hormats, "Fifty years on, we could learn still from US-China 'ping-pong diplomacy'," *The Hill*, Jan. 12, 2021, https://thehill.com/opinion/national-security/533073-fifty-years-on-we-could-learn-still-from-us-china-ping-pong.

53. "Misunderstanding China, 1972," National Archives and Records Service, Films Media Group, 2010.

54. Boyi Nan, "From a private delegation to the first imported Boeing aircraft: Shanghai's past in Sino-US exchanges," *The Paper*, Feb. 28, 2022, https://m.thepaper.cn/wifiKey_detail.jsp?contid=16869107.

55. "The Shanghai Communiqué and their lives: 50 years of Sino-US people-to-people exchanges," *The Paper*, Feb. 28, 2022, https://mil.sina.cn/zgjq/2022-02-28/detail-imcwip-ih5869452.d.html.

56. David M Lampton, *A Relationship Restored: Trends in U.S.-China Educational Exchanges, 1978-1984* (The National Academies Press, 1986).

57. Qizheng, Zhao, "From People-to-People Diplomacy to Public Diplomacy, Reflecting a Sense of Responsibility and Patrio-

tism," *People's Daily Overseas Edition*, Oct. 9, 2009, http://www.cppcc.gov.cn/2011/09/07/ARTI1315357310343515.shtml.

58. Hormats, "Fifty years on."

59. Pierre de Coubertin, "The Olympic games of 1896," *The Century Magazine*, Vol. LIII, New Series, Vol.XXXXI, Nov.1896 to Apr. 1897. Reprinted in: Norbert Müller, ed. *Pierre de Coubertin. Olympism: Selected Writings* (IOC, 2000).

60. Robert Skidelsky, "Can the Olympics Prevent War?" Project Syndicate, last modified Feb. 15, 2022, https://www.project-syndicate.org/commentary/olympic-dream-sport-politics-and-ukraine-by-robert-skidelsky-2022-02.

61. "Olympic Games: Roles and Responsibilities," IOC, accessed June 24, 2023, https://olympics.com/ioc/olympic-games-roles-and-responsibilities.

62. "Olympic Movement," IOC, accessed June 24, 2023, https://olympics.com/ioc/olympic-movement.

63. "Olympic moments when North and South Korea have marched together," Hindustan Times, accessed June 24, 2023, https://m.youtube.com/watch?v=hu-LTwDkd30.

64. "IOC Refugee Olympic Team," IOC, accessed June 24, 2023, https://olympics.com/ioc/refugee-olympic-team.

65. Lee M. Sands, "The 2008 Olympics' Impact on China," *China Business Review*, July 1, 2008, https://www.chinabusinessreview.com/the-2008-olympics-impact-on-china.

66. Liz Clarke, "Russia's anti-gay law brings controversy ahead of 2014 Sochi Olympics," *Washington Post*, Aug. 18, 2013, https://www.washingtonpost.com/sports/olympics/russias-anti-gay-law-brings-controversy-ahead-of-2014-sochi-olympics/2013/08/18/b42b5182-076f-11e3-9259-e2aafe5a5f84_story.html.

67. "Olympic Flag," Olympedia, accessed June 24, 2023, https://

www.olympedia.org/definitions/9.

68.   "Olympic Rings - Symbol of the Olympic Movement," IOC, accessed June 24, 2023, https://olympics.com/ioc/olympic-rings.

69.   "The Agitos Logo – Paralympic Symbol," IPC, accessed July 5, 2024, https://www.paralympic.org/logo.

70.   "The History of Olympic Truce," IOTC, accessed June 25, 2023, https://olympictruce.org/en/profile/history.

71.   Chunxiao Bai, "The "Olympic Truce": Past and Present," *The Paper*, Feb 4, 2022, https://m.thepaper.cn/newsDetail_forward_16478083.

72.   Malcolm Brown, *The Christmas Truce* (Macmillan, 1984).

73.   Stanley Weintraub, *Silent Night: The Story of the World War I Christmas Truce* (Plume, 2001).

74.   R. Gerald Hughes and Rachel J. Owen, "The Continuation of Politics by Other Means: Britain, the Two Germanys and the Olympic Games, 1949–1972," *Contemporary European History* 18, no 4 (2009):443-474.

75.   Carr, G.A., "The Involvement of Politics in the Sporting Relationships of East and West Germany, 1945-1972," *Journal of Sport History* 7, no. 1 (1980): 40–51.

76.   R. E. Lapchick, "A Political History of the Modern Olympic Games," *Journal of Sport and Social Issues* 2, no 1 (1978): 1-12.

77.   Erin Blakemore, "A Divided Germany Came Together for the Olympics Decades Before Korea Did," History, last modified Sep. 1, 2018, https://www.history.com/news/a-divided-germany-came-together-for-the-olympics-decades-before-korea-did.

78.   Seth Berkman, *A Team of Their Own: How an International Sisterhood Made Olympic History* (Hanover Square Press, 2019).

79.   Lucas Aykroyd, "Book: Unified Korean hockey team showed impact of sport on global issues," Global Sport Matter, last

modified Sep. 27, 2019, https://globalsportmatters.com/culture/2019/09/27/book-unified-korean-hockey-team-showed-impact-of-sport-on-global-issues.

80. Gary Waleik, "When North Joined South: The Story Of The Unified Korean Olympic Ice Hockey Team," wbur, last modified Jan. 10, 2020, https://www.wbur.org/onlyagame/2020/01/10/south-korea-north-korea-unified-hockey-pyeongchang-olympics-book.

81. Lesley Kennedy, "6 Times the Olympics Were Boycotted," History, last modified June 12, 2024, https://www.history.com/news/olympic-boycotts.

82. Tom Caraccioli, *Boycott: stolen dreams of the 1980 Moscow Olympic Games* (New Chapter Press, 2008).

83. Jessie Kratz, "Cold War Diplomatic Games: The 1984 Los Angeles Summer Olympics," National Archives, last modified Aug. 28, 2023, https://prologue.blogs.archives.gov/2023/08/28/cold-war-diplomatic-games-the-1984-los-angeles-summer-olympics.

84. "Do Sports Belong in Diplomacy?"

85. Volker Kluge, "Cancelled but Still Counted, and Never Annulled: The Games of 1916," *Journal Of Olympic History* 22, no. 2 (2014): 9-17.

86. Dave Roos, "When World Events Disrupted the Olympics," History, last modified June 12, 2024, https://www.history.com/news/olympics-postponed-cancelled.

87. David Clay Large, *Munich 1972: Tragedy, Terror, and Triumph at the Olympic Games* (Rowman & Littlefield Publishers, 2012).

88. "The United Nations and the Olympic Truce," United Nations, accessed July 23, 2024, https://www.un.org/en/olympictruce.

89. Dennis Snelling, "The Greatest Piece of Diplomacy Ever: The 1949 Tour of Lefty O'Doul and the San Francisco Seals," In

US Tours of Japan, 1907-1958 by Nichibei Yakyu (Society for American Baseball Research, 2022).

90.   Snelling, "The Greatest Piece of Diplomacy."

91.   Sayuri Guthrie-Shimizu, "For Love of the Game: Baseball in Early United States-Japanese Encounters and the Rise of a Transnational Sporting Fraternity," *Diplomatic History* 28, No. 5 (2004): 643–662.

92.   Gary T. Otake, "A Century Of Japanese American Baseball," National Japanese American Historical Society, last modified Aug. 29, 2023, https://www.njahs.org/japanese-american-baseball-history-project.

93.   "Executive Order 9066: Resulting in Japanese-American Incarceration (1942)," National Archives, accessed Jan. 24, 2024, https://www.archives.gov/milestone-documents/executive-order-9066.

94.   Bill Staples, Jr., *Kenichi Zenimura, Japanese American Baseball Pioneer* (McFarland & Company, 2011).

95.   Philip Byrd, "Baseball behind barbed wire," National Museum of American History, last modified Mar. 18, 2015, https://americanhistory.si.edu/explore/stories/baseball-behind-barbed-wire.

96.   Alex Coffey, "A field of dreams in the Arizona desert," National Baseball Hall of Fame, accessed Apr. 21, 2024, https://baseballhall.org/discover/a-field-of-dreams-in-the-arizona-desert.

97.   Terumi Rafferty-Osaki, "Sports and recreation in camp," Densho Encyclopedia, accessed Apr. 6, 2024, https://encyclopedia.densho.org/Sports_and_recreation_in_camp.

98.   Samuel O Regalado, "Sport and Community in California's Japanese American 'Yamato Colony,' 1930-1945," *Journal of Sport History* 19, no. 2 (1992): 130–43.

99. *Nikkei*, people of Japanese descent who live outside of Japan, including emigrants and their descendants born in other countries. *Issei*, first-generation Nikkei. *Nisei*, second-generation Nikkei. *Sansei*, third-generation Nikkei.

100. "To Overcome Prejudice Barriers," *Gila News Courier*, Mar. 9, 1943. https://ddr.densho.org/ddr-densho-141-65.

101. "Brooklyn Dodgers Go Liberal," *New Pittsburgh Courier*, Sep. 4, 1943, https://www.newspapers.com/article/new-pittsburgh-courier/94030084.

102. "Editorial: Huge Signs Disappeared," *Gila News Courier*, Sep. 25, 1943, https://ddr.densho.org/ddr-densho-141-158.

103. "Public Law 82-414. 1952," United States Statutes at Large 66, 163-282, June 27, 1952, https://govinfo.gov/content/pkg/STATUTE-66/pdf/STATUTE-66-Pg163.pdf.

104. Hirayama was a star athlete at Fresno State and for the Hiroshima Carp of the Nippon Professional Baseball League in Japan. Hirayama is one of the first Japanese-Americans to play in the MLB.

105. Mark Harris, "An Outfielder for Hiroshima," *Sports Illustrated*, Aug. 4, 1958, https://vault.si.com/vault/2004/09/27/playing-with-the-prose.

106. "Proclamation No. 4417. 1976," Gerald R. Ford Presidential Library & Museum, Feb. 19, 1976, https://www.fordlibrarymuseum.gov/library/speeches/760111p.htm. "Public Law 100-383. 1988," 100th Congress, Aug. 10, 1988, https://govinfo.gov/content/pkg/STATUTE-102/pdf/STATUTE-102-Pg903.pdf.

107. Joseph R. Biden, Jr., "Day Of Remembrance Of Japanese American Incarceration During World War II," The White House, Feb. 18, 2022, https://www.whitehouse.gov/briefing-room/presidential-actions/2022/02/18/day-of-remembrance-of-japanese-american-incarceration-during-world-war-ii.

108. Roger Rosenblatt, "Reflections: Why we play the game," *U.S.*

Society and Values 8, no. 2 (2003): 2-7.

109. Michael Beschloss, "For Incarcerated Japanese-Americans, Baseball Was 'Wearing the American Flag'," *New York Times*, June 20, 2014, https://www.nytimes.com/2014/06/21/upshot/for-incarcerated-japanese-americans-baseball-was-wearing-the-american-flag.html.

110. Joel Franks, *Crossing Sidelines, Crossing Cultures: Sport and Asian Pacific American Cultural Citizenship* (University Press of America, 2010).

111. "Story Behind Book Donation," *Gila News Courier*, Dec. 31, 1943, https://ddr.densho.org/ddr-densho-141-211.

112. "Two Evacuees Work for Carl Sandberg in Michigan," *Gila News Courier*, Mar. 9, 1944, https://ddr.densho.org/ddr-densho-141-241.

113. Coffey, "A field of dreams."

114. Steven Wisensale, "How Baseball Has Strengthened the Relationship Between the United States and Japan," *Smithsonian Magazine*, Mar. 29, 2018, https://www.smithsonianmag.com/history/how-baseball-strengthened-relationship-between-united-states-japan-180968597.

115. Snelling, "The Greatest Piece of Diplomacy."

116. Bunshiro Suzuki, "U.S.-Japanese Baseball and Japanese Spectators," *Yomiuri Shimbun*, Oct. 29, 1949.

117. Kyoichi Nitta, "We Learn from the Seals," *Yomiuri Shimbun*, Oct. 19, 1949.

118. "O'Doul Expresses Thanks to Japanese Fans," *Yomiuri Shimbun*, Oct. 28, 1949.

119. Nitta, "We Learn from the Seals."

120. Rob Fitts, "Joe DiMaggio's Last Hurrah: The 1951 Lefty O'Doul All-Star Tour" in Yakyu, *US Tours of Japan.*

121. Snelling, "The Greatest Piece of Diplomacy."

122. Joe Wilmot, "It All Adds Up to 'O'Douro, We Love You,'" *San Francisco Chronicle*, Feb. 6, 1950.

123. Archival materials and declassified Top Secret documents concerning Cuba and Fidel Castro can be found at https://www.jfklibrary.org/asset-viewer/archives/jfkpof-115-003#?image_identifier=JFKPOF-115-003-p0005.

124. "The Bay of Pigs," JFK Library, accessed Oct 30, 2024, https://www.jfklibrary.org/learn/about-jfk/jfk-in-history/the-bay-of-pigs.

125. "US Interests Section," US Department of State, accessed July 7, 2024, https://1997-2001.state.gov/regions/wha/cuba/usint.html.

126. Kevin Baxter, "Goodwill trip to Cuba is a big first step for baseball," *Los Angeles Times*, Dec. 17, 2015, https://www.latimes.com/sports/dodgers/la-sp-dodgers-puig-cuba-20151218-story.html.

127. Aaron Klein and Jake E. Marcus, "United States-Cuba Normalized Relations and the MLB Influence: The Baseball Coalition Committee," *The University of Miami Inter-American Law Review* 47, No. 2 (2016): 258-315.

128. Jesse Sanchez, "MLB wraps 'exhilarating' goodwill trip to Cuba," MLB, last modified Dec. 17, 2015, https://www.mlb.com/news/mlb-finishes-positive-goodwill-tour-of-cuba/c-159948056#.

129. Lou Romeo, "War in Ukraine 'stems from the Orange Revolution, a humiliating ordeal for Putin,'" France 24, last modified Feb. 26, 2023, https://www.france24.com/en/europe/20230226-war-in-ukraine-stems-from-the-orange-revolution-a-humiliating-ordeal-for-putin.

130. Nigel Walker, "Conflict in Ukraine: A timeline (current conflict, 2022 – present)," UK Parliament House of Commons Li-

brary, accessed June 16, 2024, https://commonslibrary.parliament.uk/research-briefings/cbp-9847.

131. "Ukrainian baseball team to face off against NYPD, FDNY in pair of charity games," ABC7NY, last modified Oct. 11, 2022. https://abc7ny.com/ukrainian-baseball-team-goodwill-mission-brooklyn-cyclones-manhattan/12316550.

132. "Ukrainian baseball team."

133. Nicholas McEntyre, "NYPD, FDNY to play charity baseball games against Ukraine national team," *New York Post*, Oct. 13, 2022, https://nypost.com/2022/10/13/nypd-fdny-to-play-in-charity-baseball-games-against-ukraine.

134. Nation Tricolore, "Phil Esposito's Interview 1972," last modified Feb. 3, 2011, https://www.youtube.com/watch?v=bFKvB-3Wnzgk.

135. "Strategic Arms Limitations Talks/Treaty (SALT) I and II," Office of the Historian, accessed July 1, 2023, https://history.state.gov/milestones/1969-1976/salt.

136. Robert McMahon, *Cold War: A Very Short Introduction* (Oxford University Press, 2003).

137. McMahon, *Cold War*.

138. Alex Herd, "Canada and the Cold War," Canadian Encyclopedia, last modified Jan. 21, 2022, https://www.thecanadianencyclopedia.ca/en/article/cold-war.

139. "Geneva Agreements 20-21 July 1954," United Nations, last modified July 20, 1954. https://peacemaker.un.org/sites/peacemaker.un.org/files/KH-LA   VN_540720_GenevaAgreements.pdf.

140. Herd, "Canada and the Cold War."

141. "Strategic Arms Limitations Talks."

142. McMahon, *Cold War*.

143. "Summit Series," QuantHockey, accessed Apr. 4, 2024, https://www.quanthockey.com/summit-series/en.

144. "Summit Series."

145. J. J. Wilson, "27 remarkable days: the 1972 summit series of ice hockey between Canada and the Soviet Union," *Totalitarian Movements and Political Religions* 5, no 2 (2004): 271–280.

146. "Summit Series," Hockey Hall of Fame, accessed May 21, 2024, https://www.hhof.com/hockeypedia/summitseries.html.

147. "Remembering the 1972 Summit Series, 50 years later," CBC News: The National, last modified Sep. 28, 2022, youtube.com/watch?v=6YA4mAWN_tYy.

148. "Summit Series."

149. Harry Sinden, *Hockey Showdown: The Canada-Russia Hockey Series* (Doubleday Canada, 1972).

150. Roy MacSkimming, *Cold War* (Greystone Books, 1996).

151. Cory Scurr, "Cold War by 'Other Means': Canada's Foreign Relations with Communist Eastern Europe, 1957-1963," *Theses and Dissertations (Comprehensive), 1989* (Wilfrid Laurier University Press, 2017).

152. Clem Thomas, "We had 43 million behind us," *Independent*, June 24, 1995, https://www.independent.co.uk/sport/we-had-43-million-behind-us-1588137.html.

153. Farrell Evans, "How Nelson Mandela Used Rugby as a Symbol of South African Unity," History, last modified Oct. 5, 2023, https://www.history.com/news/nelson-mandela-1995-rugby-world-cup-south-african-unity.

154. "South Africa profile – Timeline," BBC, last modified 19 Dec. 2022, https://www.bbc.com/news/world-africa-14094918.

155. Robert Ross, *A Concise History of South Africa* (Cambridge University Press, 1999).

156. Peter Walshe, *The Rise of Nationalism in South Afraid: The African National Congress, 1912-195* (Hurst, 1970).

157. Anthony W. Marx, *Lessons of Struggle: South African Internal Opposition, 1960- 1990* (Oxford University Press, 1992).

158. "Nelson Mandela sentenced to life imprisonment 44 years ago," Nelson Mandela Foundation, last modified June 11, 2008, https://www.nelsonmandela.org/news/entry/nelson-mandela-sentenced-to-life-imprisonment-44-years-ago.

159. Tom Lodge, *Mandela: A Critical Life* (Oxford University Press, 2006).

160. Lodge, *Mandela*.

161. Lodge, *Mandela*.

162. "International Convention on the Suppression and Punishment of the Crime of Apartheid," United Nations, entered into force July 18, 1976, https://www.un.org/en/genocideprevention/documents/atrocitycrimes/Doc.10_International%20Convention%20on%20the%20Suppression%20and%20Punishment%20of%20the%20Crime%20of%20Apartheid.pdf.

163. Thomas, "We had 43 million."

164. David Taylor, "Iran vs USA and the most political moments in World Cup history," *GQ Magazine*, Nov. 29, 2022, https://www.gq-magazine.co.uk/sport/gallery/most-political-moments-in-world-cup-history.

165. Chris Evans, "'I'd make it more political': when USA lost to Iran at the World Cup in 1998," *The Guardian*, Nov. 29, 2022, https://theguardian.com/football/2022/nov/29/iran-players-usa-world-cup-98-steve-sampson-player-alexi-lalas.

166. "Politics in Football: USA vs Iran in '98," FIFA Museum, last modified Apr. 8, 2016, https://www.fifamuseum.

com/en/blog-stories/blog/politics-in-football-iran-vs-usa-in-98-2611344.

167. Sean Gregory, "Iran Stunned the U.S. at the 1998 World Cup. That Game Offers Lessons For a Monumental Rematch in Qatar," *Time*, Nov. 25, 2022, https://time.com/6236735/world-cup-usa-iran-lessons.

168. Bernd Debusmann, Jr., "World Cup Iran-US: Why Iran gave the US players flowers in 1998," BBC, last modified Nov. 29, 2022, https://www.bbc.com/news/world-us-canada-63797316.

169. Nick Dall, "India-Pakistan rivalry: Whatever happened to 'cricket diplomacy'?" Al Jazeera, last modified Oct. 11, 2023, https://www.aljazeera.com/sports/2023/10/11/cricket-diplomacy-icc-world-cup-2023-india-pakistan-south-africa.

170. T.V. Paul, ed., *The India-Pakistan Conflict: An Enduring Rivalry* (Cambridge University Press, 2005).

171. Paul, ed., *The India-Pakistan Conflict*.

172. Paul, ed., *The India-Pakistan Conflict*.

173. Sumit Ganguly, *Deadly Impasse: Indo-Pakistani Relations at the Dawn of a New Century* (Cambridge University Press, 2016).

174. Paul, ed., *The India-Pakistan Conflict*.

175. Ganguly, *Deadly Impasse*.

176. Paul, ed., *The India-Pakistan Conflict*.

177. Bruce Riedel, "Mumbai Attacks: Four Years Later," Bookings, last modified Nov. 26, 2012, https://www.brookings.edu/articles/mumbai-attacks-four-years-later.

178. Ganguly, *Deadly Impasse*.

179. Helen Regan, Nikhil Kumar and Sophia Saifi, "Pakistan vows retaliation after Indian airstrikes, as hostilities rise between nuclear powers," CNN, last modified Feb. 26, 2019, https://www.cnn.com/2019/02/26/india/india-pakistan-line-of-con-

trol-incursion-intl/index.html.

180. Sebastian, Meryl and Sharanya Hrishikesh, "Article 370: India Supreme Court upholds repeal of Kashmir's special status," BBC News, last modified Dec. 11, 2023, https://www.bbc.com/news/world-asia-india-67634689.

181. Martand Jha, "India and Pakistan's Cricket Diplomacy," *The Diplomat*, March 15, 2017, https://thediplomat.com/2017/03/india-and-pakistans-cricket-diplomacy.

182. Jha, "India and Pakistan's Cricket Diplomacy."

183. Jannatul Naym Pieal, "Is India-Pakistan 'cricket diplomacy' still a thing?" The Business Standard, last modified October 14, 2023, https://www.tbsnews.net/sports/india-pakistan-cricket-diplomacy-still-thing-718142.

184. Jha, "India and Pakistan's Cricket Diplomacy."

185. Pieal, "Is India-Pakistan."

186. "Do Sports Belong in Diplomacy?"

187. "National Basketball Association (NBA)," NBA, accessed Aug. 25, 2024, https://careers.nba.com/ourleagues/#:~:text=Built%20around%20five%20professional%20sports,-sale%20in%20more%20than%20200.

188. Fran Blinebury, "Basketball has become 'part of the Chinese culture'," NBA, last modified Oct. 8, 2016, https://www.nba.com/news/nba-and-china-growing-relationship.

189. Michael Lee, "The NBA in China: Opening a Super Market," *Washington Post*, October 18, 2007, http://www.washingtonpost.com/wpdyn/content/article/2007/10/17/AR2007101702218.html.

190. Ben Sin, "NBA Looks to Asia for Next Growth Spurt," *New York Times*, March 14, 2014, http://www.nytimes.com/2014/03/15/business/international/nba-looks-to-asia-for-next-growth-spurt.html.

191. Haozhou Pu, "Mediating the giants: Yao Ming, NBA and the cultural politics of Sino-American relations," *Asia Pacific Journal of Sport and Social Science* 5, no 2 (2016): 87–107.

192. Liangjun Zhou, Jerred Junqi Wang, Xiaoying Chen, Chundong Lei, James J. Zhang and Xiao Meng, "The development of NBA in China: a glocalization perspective," *International Journal of Sports Marketing and Sponsorship* 18, no 1 (2017): 81-94.

193. May Zhou, "NBA does a slam-dunk in China," *China Daily*, April 4, 2014, http://usa.chinadaily.com.cn/epaper/2014-04/04/content_17409032.htm.

194. Nectar Gan and Emiko Jozuka, "Chinese fans in mourning: Kobe Bryant's death draws an outpouring of shock and grief," CNN, last modified Jan. 27, 2020, https://www.cnn.com/2020/01/27/asia/asia-mourns-kobe-bryant-intl-hnk/index.html.

195. "North Korea and Harlem Globetrotters' Diplomacy Basketball Lunch (VICE on HBO)," VICE, last modified June 14, 2013, https://www.youtube.com/watch?v=BoeSlDeb3NY.

196. Helena Andrews-Dyer, "A brief guide to Dennis Rodman's long, weird history with North Korea," *Washington Post*, June 12, 2018, https://www.washingtonpost.com/news/reliable-source/wp/2018/06/12/a-brief-guide-to-dennis-rodmans-long-weird-history-with-north-korea.

197. "From the Pitch to Power: Three Athletes Who Made the Transition from Sport to Politics," Sprter, last modified April 5, 2018, https://sprter.com/uncategorized/athletes-in-politics.

198. Deborah Riley Draper, Blair Underwood, and Travis Thrasher, *Olympic Pride, American Prejudice: The Untold Story of 18 African Americans Who Defied Jim Crow and Adolf Hitler to Compete in the 1936 Berlin Olympics* (Atria Books, 2020).

199. Tony Gentry and Heather Lehr Wagner, *Jesse Owens: Champi-*

on Athlete (Chelsea House Publishers, 2005).

200. Rahul Mukherji, "Friendship of Luz Long and Jesse Owens from 1936 Berlin Olympic Games," The International Platform on Sport and Development, last modified May 23. 2023, https://www.sportanddev.org/latest/news/friendship-luz-long-and-jesse-owens-1936-berlin-olympic-games.

201. Dave Roos, "'Blood in the Water': The Cold War Olympic Showdown Between Hungary and the USSR," History, last modified June 4. 2021, https://www.history.com/news/blood-in-the-water-1956-olympic-water-polo-hungary-ussr.

202. Miles Corwin, "Blood in the Water at the 1956 Olympics," *Smithsonian Magazine*, July 31, 2008, https://www.smithsonianmag.com/history/blood-in-the-water-at-the-1956-olympics-1616787.

203. Lewis A. Erenberg, *The rumble in the jungle: Muhammad Ali and George Foreman on the global stage* (University of Chicago Press, 2019).

204. Josh Peter, "Revisiting 'The Rumble in the Jungle' 40 years later," *USA TODAY Sports*, Oct 29, 2014, https://www.usatoday.com/story/sports/boxing/2014/10/29/muhammad-ali-george-foreman-rumble-in-the-jungle-40th-anniversary/18097587.

205. Mike Eruzione and Neal Boudette, *The Making of a Miracle: The Untold Story of the Captain of the 1980 Gold Medal–Winning U.S. Olympic Hockey Team* (Harper, 2020).

206. Michael Burgan, *Miracle on Ice: How a Stunning Upset United a Country* (Compass Point Books, 2016).

207. Brian Trusdell, *Miracle on Ice.*

208. Eruzione and Boudette, *The Making of a Miracle.*

209. Felipe Cardenas, "The origins of the Hand of God, a goal still contentious two years after Maradona's death," *New York Times*, Dec. 16, 2022, https://www.nytimes.com/athlet-

ic/3984530/2022/12/16/hand-of-god-maradona-world-cup.

210. Stefan Szymanski, "Why Maradona's 'Hand of God' goal is priceless – and unforgettable," *The Conversation*, Nov. 19, 2022, https://theconversation.com/why-maradonas-hand-of-god-goal-is-priceless-and-unforgettable-193760.

211. Usain Bolt, *The Fastest Man Alive: The True Story of Usain Bolt* (Sports Publishing, 2016).

212. Berris, Hoarfrost, and Spelman, "Celebrating the 50th Anniversary."

213. Berris, Hoarfrost, and Spelman, "Celebrating the 50th Anniversary."

214. "Sports Diplomacy," Bureau of Educational and Cultural Affairs, accessed July 7, 2024, https://eca.state.gov/sports-diplomacy.

215. "International Inspiration," British Council, accessed July 7, 2024. https://www.britishcouncil.org/society/sport/current-programmes/international-inspiration.

216. "Sport for Tomorrow," JapanGov, accessed July 7, 2024, https://www.japan.go.jp/tomodachi/2018/winter2018/sport_for_tomorrow.html.

217. "Australian Sports Commission - Sport for Development," Australian Government, Ausport, accessed July 7, 2024, https://www.ausport.gov.au.

218. "Restart Series On Democracy Promotion Launched," German Olympic Sports Confederation (DOSB), accessed July 7, 2024, https://www.dosb.de/sonderseiten/news/news-detail/news/restart-themenreihe-demokratiefoerderung-erfolgreich-gestartet.

219. Janine Romero Valenzuela, "Integration through sports," Global Compact on Refugees, accessed July 7, 2024, https://globalcompactrefugees.org/good-practices/integra-

tion-through-sports.

220. Regan, Kumar and Saifi, "Pakistan vows."

221. Berris, Hoarfrost, and Spelman, "Celebrating the 50th Anniversary."

Bibliography

ABC7NY. "Ukrainian baseball team to face off against NYPD, FDNY in pair of charity games." Last modified Oct. 11, 2022. https://abc7ny.com/ukrainian-baseball-team-goodwill-mission-brooklyn-cyclones-manhattan/12316550.

Albert, Eleanor. "The Mixed Record of Sports Diplomacy, Council on Foreign Relations." Council on Foreign Relations, last modified Feb. 6, 2018. https://www.cfr.org/interview/mixed-record-sports-diplomacy.

Andrews, Evan. "How Ping-Pong Diplomacy Thawed the Cold War." History, last modified Oct. 19, 2018. https://www.history.com/news/ping-pong-diplomacy.

Andrews-Dyer, Helena. "A brief guide to Dennis Rodman's long, weird history with North Korea." *Washington Post*, June 12, 2018. https://www.washingtonpost.com/news/reliable-source/wp/2018/06/12/a-brief-guide-to-dennis-rodmans-long-weird-history-with-north-korea.

Ausport. "Australian Sports Commission - Sport for Development." Australian Government. Accessed July 7, 2024. https://www.ausport.gov.au.

Aykroyd, Lucas. "Book: Unified Korean hockey team showed impact of sport on global issues." *Global Sport Matters*, Sep. 27, 2019. https://globalsportmatters.com/culture/2019/09/27/book-unified-korean-hockey-team-showed-impact-of-sport-on-global-issues.

Bai, Chunxiao. "The 'Olympic Truce': Past and Present." *The Paper*, Feb 4, 2022. https://m.thepaper.cn/newsDetail_forward_16478083.

Baxter, Kevin. "Goodwill trip to Cuba is a big first step for baseball." *Los Angeles Times*, Dec. 17, 2015. https://www.latimes.com/sports/dodgers/la-sp-dodgers-puig-cuba-20151218-story.

html.

BBC. "South Africa profile - Timeline." Last modified Dec. 19, 2022. https://www.bbc.com/news/world-africa-14094918.

Berkman, Seth. *A Team of Their Own: How an International Sisterhood Made Olympic History*. Hanover Square Press, 2019.

Berris, Jan, Judy Hoarfrost, and Doug Spelman. "Celebrating the 50th Anniversary of Ping Pong Diplomacy." Hosted by the National Committee on U.S.-China Relations on Apr. 28, 2021. Video, 37:49. https://www.youtube.com/watch?v=E-jAV0D5FwW8.

Beschloss, Michael. "For Incarcerated Japanese-Americans, Baseball Was 'Wearing the American Flag'." *New York Times*, June 20, 2014. https://www.nytimes.com/2014/06/21/upshot/for-incarcerated-japanese-americans-baseball-was-wearing-the-american-flag.html.

Biden, Joseph R, Jr. "Day Of Remembrance Of Japanese American Incarceration During World War II." The White House, last modified Feb. 18, 2022. https://www.whitehouse.gov/briefing-room/presidential-actions/2022/02/18/day-of-remembrance-of-japanese-american-incarceration-during-world-war-ii.

Blakemore, Erin. "A Divided Germany Came Together for the Olympics Decades Before Korea Did." History. Last Modified Sep. 1, 2018. https://www.history.com/news/a-divided-germany-came-together-for-the-olympics-decades-before-korea-did.

Blinebury, Fran. "Basketball has become 'part of the Chinese culture'." NBA. Last modified Oct. 8, 2016. https://www.nba.com/news/nba-and-china-growing-relationship.

Bolt, Usain. *The Fastest Man Alive: The True Story of Usain Bolt*. Sports Publishing, 2016.

Bridges, Brian. "Driver of Peace? Ping-Pong Diplomacy on The Korean Peninsula." *International Journal of Korean History* 25, No. 2 (2020): 75-102.

British Council. "International Inspiration." Accessed July 7, 2024. https://www.britishcouncil.org/society/sport/current-pro-grammes/international-inspiration.

"Brooklyn Dodgers Go Liberal." *New Pittsburgh Courier*, Sep. 4, 1943. https://www.newspapers.com/article/new-pittsburgh-cou-rier/94030084.

Brown, Malcolm. *The Christmas Truce*. Macmillan, 1984.

Bureau of Educational and Cultural Affairs. "Sports Diplomacy." Accessed July 7, 2024. https://eca.state.gov/sports-diplomacy.

Burgan, Michael. *Miracle on Ice: How a Stunning Upset United a Country*. Compass Point Books, 2016.

Burr, William. "The Beijing-Washington Back-Channel and Henry Kissinger's Secret Trip to China." National Security Archive Electronic Briefing Book No. 66. The National Security Archive, Feb. 27, 2002. https://nsarchive2.gwu.edu/NSAEBB/NSAEBB66.

Byrd, Philip. "Baseball behind barbed wire." National Museum of American History. Last modified Mar. 18, 2015. https://americanhistory.si.edu/explore/stories/baseball-behind-barbed-wire.

Caraccioli, Tom. *Boycott: stolen dreams of the 1980 Moscow Olympic Games*. New Chapter Press, 2008.

Cardenas, Felipe. "The origins of the Hand of God, a goal still contentious two years after Maradona's death." *New York Times*, Dec. 16, 2022. https://www.nytimes.com/athletic/3984530/2022/12/16/hand-of-god-maradona-world-cup.

Carr, G.A. "The Involvement of Politics in the Sporting Relationships of East and West Germany, 1945-1972." *Journal of Sport History* 7, no. 1 (1980): 40–51.

CBC News. "Remembering the 1972 Summit Series, 50 years later." Last modified Sep. 28, 2022. youtube.com/watch?v=6YA-4mAWN_tYy.

Chang, Jung and Jon Halliday. *Mao: The Unknown Story*. Jonathan Cape, 2005.

Clarke, Liz. "Russia's anti-gay law brings controversy ahead of 2014 Sochi Olympics." *Washington Post,* Aug. 18, 2013. https://www.washingtonpost.com/sports/olympics/russias-anti-gay-law-brings-controversy-ahead-of-2014-sochi-olympics/2013/08/18/b42b5182-076f-11e3-9259-e2aafe5a5f84_story.html.

Coffey, Alex. "A field of dreams in the Arizona desert," National Baseball Hall of Fame. Accessed Apr. 21, 2024. https://baseballhall.org/discover/a-field-of-dreams-in-the-arizona-desert.

Corwin, Miles. "Blood in the Water at the 1956 Olympics." *Smithsonian Magazine,* July 31, 2008. https://www.smithsonianmag.com/history/blood-in-the-water-at-the-1956-olympics-1616787.

Coubertin, Pierre. "The Olympic games of 1896." *The Century Magazine,* Vol. LIII, New Series, Vol. XXXXI, Nov.1896 to Apr. 1897. Reprinted in: Norbert Müller, ed. *Pierre de Coubertin. Olympism: Selected Writings.* IOC, 2000.

Dall, Nick. "India-Pakistan rivalry: Whatever happened to 'cricket diplomacy'?" Al Jazeera. Last modified Oct. 11, 2023. https://www.aljazeera.com/sports/2023/10/11/cricket-diplomacy-icc-world-cup-2023-india-pakistan-south-africa.

Debusmann, Bernd, Jr. "World Cup Iran-US: Why Iran gave the US players flowers in 1998." BBC. Last modified Nov. 29, 2022. https://www.bbc.com/news/world-us-canada-63797316.

DeHart, Jonathan. "The Legacy of Ping-Pong Diplomat Zhuang Zedong." *The Diplomat,* Feb. 13, 2013. https://thediplomat.com/2013/02/the-legacy-of-ping-pong-diplomat-zhuang-zedong.

Draper, Deborah Riley, Blair Underwood, and Travis Thrasher. *Olympic Pride, American Prejudice: The Untold Story of 18 African Americans Who Defied Jim Crow and Adolf Hitler to Compete in the 1936 Berlin Olympics.* Atria Books, 2020.

Duke Today. "Do Sports Belong in Diplomacy? What Leaders from the NBA, Olympics and College Think." Last modified Sep.

29, 2023. https://today.duke.edu/2023/09/do-sports-belong-diplomacy-what-leaders-nba-olympics-and-college-think.

"Editorial: Huge Signs Disappeared." 1943. *Gila News Courier*, Sep. 25, 1943. https://ddr.densho.org/ddr-densho-141-158.

Erenberg, Lewis A. *The rumble in the jungle: Muhammad Ali and George Foreman on the global stage.* University of Chicago Press, 2019.

Eruzione, Mike and Neal Boudette. *The Making of a Miracle: The Untold Story of the Captain of the 1980 Gold Medal–Winning U.S. Olympic Hockey Team.* Harper, 2020.

Evans, Chris. "'I'd make it more political': when USA lost to Iran at the World Cup in 1998." *The Guardian*, Nov. 29, 2022. https://theguardian.com/football/2022/nov/29/iran-players-usa-world-cup-98-steve-sampson-player-alexi-lalas.

Evans, Farrell. "How Nelson Mandela Used Rugby as a Symbol of South African Unity." History. Last modified Oct. 5, 2023. https://www.history.com/news/nelson-mandela-1995-rugby-world-cup-south-african-unity.

Facts and Details. "Ping Pong Diplomacy And Secret Henry Kissinger Visits To China." Last modified Aug. 2021. https://factsanddetails.com/china/cat2/sub6/entry-5535.html.

FIFA Museum. "Politics in Football: USA vs Iran in '98." Last modified Apr. 8, 2016. https://www.fifamuseum.com/en/blog-stories/blog/politics-in-football-iran-vs-usa-in-98-2611344

Fitts, Rob. "Joe DiMaggio's Last Hurrah: The 1951 Lefty O'Doul All-Star Tour," in Nichibei Yakyu: *US Tours of Japan, 1907-1958*. Society for American Baseball Research, 2022.

Franks, Joel. *Crossing Sidelines, Crossing Cultures: Sport and Asian Pacific American Cultural Citizenship.* University Press of America, 2010.

Gan, Nectar and Emiko Jozuka. "Chinese fans in mourning: Kobe Bryant's death draws an outpouring of shock and grief." CNN. Last modified Jan. 27, 2020. https://www.cnn.com/2020/01/27/asia/asia-mourns-kobe-bryant-intl-hnk/

index.html.

Ganguly, Sumit. *Deadly Impasse: Indo-Pakistani Relations at the Dawn of a New Century*. Cambridge University Press, 2016.

Gentry, Tony and Heather Lehr Wagner. *Jesse Owens: Champion Athlete*. Chelsea House Publishers, 2005.

German Olympic Sports Confederation (DOSB). "Restart Series On Democracy Promotion Launched." Accessed July 7, 2024. https://www.dosb.de/sonderseiten/news/news-detail/news/restart-themenreihe-demokratiefoerderung-erfolgreich-gestartet.

Gregory, Sean. "Iran Stunned the U.S. at the 1998 World Cup. That Game Offers Lessons For a Monumental Rematch in Qatar." *Time*, Nov. 25, 2022. https://time.com/6236735/world-cup-usa-iran-lessons.

Guthrie-Shimizu, Sayuri. "For Love of the Game: Baseball in Early United States-Japanese Encounters and the Rise of a Transnational Sporting Fraternity," *Diplomatic History* 28, No. 5 (2004): 643–662.

Harris, Mark. "An Outfielder for Hiroshima." *Sports Illustrated*, Aug. 4, 1958. https://vault.si.com/vault/2004/09/27/playing-with-the-prose.

Herd, Alex. "Canada and the Cold War." The Canadian Encyclopedia. Last modified Jan. 21, 2022. https://www.thecanadianencyclopedia.ca/en/article/cold-war.

Hindustan Times. "Olympic moments when North and South Korea have marched together." Accessed June 24, 2023. https://m.youtube.com/watch?v=hu-LTwDkd30.

Hockey Hall of Fame. "Summit Series." Accessed May 21, 2024. https://www.hhof.com/hockeypedia/summitseries.html.

Hormats, Robert. "Fifty years on, we could learn still from US-China 'ping-pong diplomacy'." *The Hill*, Jan. 12, 2021. https://thehill.com/opinion/national-security/533073-fifty-years-on-we-could-learn-still-from-us-china-ping-pong.

Hughes, R. Gerald and Rachel J. Owen. "The Continuation of Politics by Other Means: Britain, the Two Germanys and the Olympic Games, 1949–1972." *Contemporary European History* 18, no 4 (2009):443-474.

IOC. "IOC Refugee Olympic Team." Accessed June 24, 2023. https://olympics.com/ioc/refugee-olympic-team.

IOC. "Olympic Games: Roles and Responsibilities." Accessed June 24, 2023. https://olympics.com/ioc/olympic-games-roles-and-responsibilities.

IOC. "Olympic Movement." Accessed June 24, 2023. https://olympics.com/ioc/olympic-movement.

IOC. "Olympic Rings - Symbol of the Olympic Movement." Accessed June 24, 2023. https://olympics.com/ioc/olympic-rings.

IOTC. "The History of Olympic Truce." Accessed June 25, 2023. https://olympictruce.org/en/profile/history.

IPC. "The Agitos Logo – Paralympic Symbol." Accessed July 5, 2024. https://www.paralympic.org/logo.

Itoh, Mayumi. *The Origin of Ping-Pong Diplomacy: The Forgotten Architect of Sino-U.S. Rapprochement.* Palgrave Macmillan, 2011.

JapanGov. "Sport for Tomorrow." Accessed July 7, 2024. https://www.japan.go.jp/tomodachi/2018/winter2018/sport_for_tomorrow.html.

JFK Library. "The Bay of Pigs." Accessed July 20, 2023. https://www.jfklibrary.org/learn/about-jfk/jfk-in-history/the-bay-of-pigs.

Jha, Martand. "India and Pakistan's Cricket Diplomacy." *The Diplomat,* March 15, 2017. https://thediplomat.com/2017/03/india-and-pakistans-cricket-diplomacy.

Joint Communique. "Joint Communique between the United States and China." Wilson Center. Last modified Feb. 28, 1972. https://digitalarchive.wilsoncenter.org/document/joint-communique-between-united-states-and-china.

Kennedy, Lesley. "6 Times the Olympics Were Boycotted." History. Last modified June 12, 2024. https://www.history.com/news/olympic-boycotts.

Kissinger, Henry A. "My talk with Chou En-lai." USC US-China

Institute. Last modified July 14, 1971. china.usc.edu/sites/default/files/article/attachments/19710714-kissinger-to-nixon-on-secret-meetings-in-china.pdf.

Klein, Aaron and Jake E. Marcus. "United States-Cuba Normalized Relations and the MLB Influence: The Baseball Coalition Committee." *The University of Miami Inter-American Law Review* 47, No. 2 (2016): 258-315.

Kluge, Volker. "Cancelled but Still Counted, and Never Annulled: The Games of 1916." *Journal Of Olympic History* 22, no. 2 (2014): 9-17.

Kratz, Jessie. "Cold War Diplomatic Games: The 1984 Los Angeles Summer Olympics." National Archives. Last modified Aug. 28, 2023. https://prologue.blogs.archives.gov/2023/08/28/cold-war-diplomatic-games-the-1984-los-angeles-summer-olympics.

Lampton, David M. *A Relationship Restored: Trends in U.S.-China Educational Exchanges, 1978-1984.* The National Academies Press, 1986.

Lapchick, R. E. "A Political History of the Modern Olympic Games." *Journal of Sport and Social Issues* 2, no 1 (1978): 1-12.

Large, David Clay. *Munich 1972: Tragedy, Terror, and Triumph at the Olympic Games.* Rowman & Littlefield Publishers, 2012.

Lee, Michael. "The NBA in China: Opening a Super Market." *Washington Post,* October 18, 2007. http://www.washingtonpost.com/wpdyn/content/article/2007/10/17/AR2007101702218.html.

Li, Hongshan. *Fighting on the Cultural Front: U.S.-China Relations in the Cold War.* Columbia University Press, 2024.

Lodge, Tom. *Mandela: A Critical Life.* Oxford University Press, 2006.

Mandela, Nelson. "Sport has the power to change the world." Laureus Lifetime Achievement Award Speech. Accessed Mar. 25, 2022. https://www.laureus.com/about.

Marx, Anthony W. *Lessons of Struggle: South African Internal Opposition, 1960- 1990.* Oxford University Press, 1992.

McEntyre, Nicholas. "NYPD, FDNY to play charity baseball games against Ukraine national team." *New York Post*, Oct. 13, 2022. https://nypost.com/2022/10/13/nypd-fdny-to-play-in-charity-baseball-games-against-ukraine.

McMahon, Robert. *Cold War: A Very Short Introduction.* Oxford University Press, 2003.

Millwood, Pete. "An 'Exceedingly Delicate Undertaking': Sino-American Science Diplomacy, 1966–78." *Journal of Contemporary History* 56, no 1 (2021): 166-190.

Ministry of Foreign Affairs of China. "List of countries with which China has diplomatic relations." Accessed June 23, 2023. https://www.mfa.gov.cn/web/zili-ao_674904/2193_674977/200812/t20081221_9284708.shtml.

MLB. "MLB players to participate in Cuba goodwill tour Dec.15-18." Last modified Dec. 3, 2015. https://www.mlb.com/news/mlb-players-to-participate-in-cuba-goodwill-tour-dec-15-18/c-158751058.

Mukherji, Rahul. "Friendship of Luz Long and Jesse Owens from 1936 Berlin Olympic Games." The International Platform on Sport and Development. Last modified May 23. 2023. https://www.sportanddev.org/latest/news/friendship-luz-long-and-jesse-owens-1936-berlin-olympic-games.

Nan, Boyi. "From a private delegation to the first imported Boeing aircraft: Shanghai's past in Sino-US exchanges." *The Paper*, Feb. 28, 2022. https://m.thepaper.cn/wifiKey_detail.jsp?-contid=16869107.

National Archives. "Executive Order 9066: Resulting in Japanese-American Incarceration (1942)." Accessed Jan. 24, 2024. https://www.archives.gov/milestone-documents/executive-order-9066.

National Archives. Nixon Presidential Materials, NSC Files, Box 1319, NSC Unfiled Material, 1969, 1 of 19. White House Special Files, President's Office Files, Box 1, President's handwriting File, January 1969. Last modified Feb. 1, 1969. history.state.gov/historicaldocuments/frus1969-76v17/d3.

National Archives and Records Service. *Misunderstanding China,*

1972. Films Media Group, 2010.

National Museum of American Diplomacy. "Ping-Pong Diplomacy: Artifacts from the Historic 1971 U.S. Table Tennis Trip to China." Last modified August 5, 2021. https://diplomacy. state.gov/ping-pong-diplomacy-historic-1971-u-s-table-tennis-trip-to-china.

Nation Tricolore. "Phil Esposito's Interview 1972." Last modified Feb. 3, 2011. https://www.youtube.com/watch?v=bFKvB-3Wnzgk.

NBA. "National Basketball Association (NBA)." Accessed Aug. 25, 2024. https://careers.nba.com/ourleagues/#:~:text=Built%20around%20five%20professional%20sports,-sale%20in%20more%20than%20200.

Nelson Mandela Foundation. "Nelson Mandela sentenced to life imprisonment 44 years ago." Last modified June 11, 2008. https://www.nelsonmandela.org/news/entry/nelson-mandela-sentenced-to-life-imprisonment-44-years-ago.

Nitta, Kyoichi. 1949. "We Learn from the Seals." *Yomiuri Shimbun*, Oct. 19, 1949.

Nixon, Richard. "Foundations of Foreign Policy, 1969-1972." *Foreign Affairs* 46, No. 1 (1967): 113-125.

Nixon, Richard. "Remarks to the Nation Announcing Acceptance of an Invitation To Visit the People's Republic of China." The American Presidency Project. Last modified July 15, 1971. https://www.presidency.ucsb.edu/documents/remarks-the-nation-announcing-acceptance-invitation-visit-the-peoples-republic-china.

Nixon, Richard. *RN: The Memoirs of Richard Nixon*. Simon & Schuster, 1990.

Office of the Historian. "Strategic Arms Limitations Talks/Treaty (SALT) I and II." Accessed July 1, 2023. https://history.state. gov/milestones/1969-1976/salt.

Office of the Historian. "Wartime Conferences, 1941–1945." Accessed July 1, 2023. https://history.state.gov/milestones/1937-1945/war-time-conferences.

Olympedia. "1984 Summer Olympics." Accessed June 22, 2023. https://www.olympedia.org/editions/21.

Olympedia. "Olympic Flag." Accessed June 24, 2023. https://www.olympedia.org/definitions/9.

Otake, Gary T. "A Century Of Japanese American Baseball," National Japanese American Historical Society. Last modified Aug. 29, 2023. https://www.njahs.org/japanese-american-baseball-history-project.

Owen, David. "Hello China! Ping-pong diplomacy and the value of spontaneity when building bridges through sport." Inside the Games. Last modified Apr. 14, 2021. https://www.insidethegames.biz/articles/1106599/ping-pong-diplomacy-china-sport.

Palmeri, Tara. "Kim Jong Un wanted 'famous' US basketball players as part of denuclearization deal: Sources." ABC News. Last modified May 9, 2019. https://abcnews.go.com/Politics/kim-jong-wanted-famous-us-basketball-players-part/story?id=62920773#.

Paul, T.V., ed. *The India-Pakistan Conflict: An Enduring Rivalry*. Cambridge University Press, 2005.

PBS. "Nixon's China Game Timeline." Accessed June 3, 2023. https://www.pbs.org/wgbh/americanexperience/features/china-timeline.

PBS. "Ping Pong Diplomacy." Accessed July 4, 2023. https://www.pbs.org/wgbh/americanexperience/features/china-ping-pong.

Peter, Josh. "Revisiting 'The Rumble in the Jungle' 40 years later." *USA TODAY Sports*, Oct 29, 2014. https://www.usatoday.com/story/sports/boxing/2014/10/29/muhammad-ali-george-foreman-rumble-in-the-jungle-40th-anniversary/18097587.

Pieal, Jannatul Naym. "Is India-Pakistan 'cricket diplomacy' still a thing?" The Business Standard. Last modified October 14, 2023. https://www.tbsnews.net/sports/india-pakistan-cricket-diplomacy-still-thing-718142.

"Proclamation No. 4417. 1976." Gerald R. Ford Presidential Library & Museum. Last modified Feb. 19, 1976. https://www.ford-librarymuseum.gov/library/speeches/760111p.htm.

"Public Law 82-414. 1952." United States Statutes at Large 66, 163-282, June 27, 1952. https://govinfo.gov/content/pkg/STAT-UTE-66/pdf/STATUTE-66-Pg163.pdf.

"Public Law 100-383. 1988." 100th Congress, Aug. 10, 1988. https://govinfo.gov/content/pkg/STATUTE-102/pdf/STATUTE-102-Pg903.pdf.

Pu, Haozhou. "Mediating the giants: Yao Ming, NBA and the cultural politics of Sino-American relations." *Asia Pacific Journal of Sport and Social Science* 5, no 2 (2016): 87–107.

QuantHockey. "Summit Series." Accessed Apr. 4, 2024. https://www.quanthockey.com/summit-series/en.

Rafferty-Osaki, Terumi. "Sports and recreation in camp," Densho Encyclopedia. Last modified Apr. 6, 2024. https://encyclopedia.densho.org/Sports_and_recreation_in_camp.

Reagan, Ronald. "Remarks at Fudan University in Shanghai, China." Ronald Reagan Presidential Libraries and Museum, 30 April 1984. https://www.reaganlibrary.gov/archives/speech/remarks-fudan-universityshanghai-china.

Regalado, Samuel O. "Sport and Community in California's Japanese American 'Yamato Colony,' 1930-1945," *Journal of Sport History* 19, no. 2 (1992): 130–43.

Regan, Helen, Nikhil Kumar and Sophia Saifi. "Pakistan vows retaliation after Indian airstrikes, as hostilities rise between nuclear powers." CNN. Last modified Feb. 26, 2019. https://www.cnn.com/2019/02/26/india/india-pakistan-line-of-control-incursion-intl/index.html.

Richard Nixon Foundation. "41 Years Ago – The Week that Changed the World." Last modified Feb. 21, 2013. https://www.nixonfoundation.org/2013/02/41-years-ago-the-week-that-changed-the-world.

Richard Nixon Foundation. "Nixon Legacy Forum Transcript: The Opening to China: A Discussion with Henry Kissinger."

Last modified March 7, 2012. https://www.nixonfounda-tion.org/wp-content/uploads/2019/04/Nixon-Legacy-Fo-rum-A-Discussion-With-Henry-Kissinger-on-The-Opening-to-China.pdf.

Riedel, Bruce. "Mumbai Attacks: Four Years Later." Bookings. Last modified Nov. 26, 2012. https://www.brookings.edu/arti-cles/mumbai-attacks-four-years-later.

Roberts, Steven V. "'Ping-pong Diplomacy: The Secret History Behind the Game That Changed the World' by Nicholas Griffin." *Washington Post*, Jan. 24, 2014. https://www.washingtonpost.com/opinions/ping-pong-diplomacy-the-secret-history-behind-the-game-that-changed-the-world-by-nicholas-griffin/2014/01/24/03e10536-794f-11e3-af7f-13bf0e9965f6_story.html.

Robles, Frances and Julie Hirschfeld Davis. "U.S. Frees Last of the 'Cuban Five,' Part of a 1990s Spy Ring." *New York Times*, Dec. 17, 2014. https://www.nytimes.com/2014/12/18/world/americas/us-frees-last-of-the-cuban-five-part-of-a-1990s-spy-ring-.html.

Romeo, Lou. "War in Ukraine 'stems from the Orange Revolu-tion, a humiliating ordeal for Putin'." France 24. Last modified Feb. 26, 2023. https://www.france24.com/en/europe/20230226-war-in-ukraine-stems-from-the-orange-revolution-a-humiliating-ordeal-for-putin.

Roos, Dave. "'Blood in the Water': The Cold War Olympic Show-down Between Hungary and the USSR." History. Last modified June 4. 2021. https://www.history.com/news/blood-in-the-water-1956-olympic-water-polo-hungary-ussr.

Roos, Dave. "When World Events Disrupted the Olympics." History. Last modified June 12, 2024. https://www.history.com/news/olympics-postponed-cancelled.

Rosenblatt, Roger. "Reflections: Why we play the game." *U.S. Society and Values* 8, no. 2 (2003): 2-7.

Ross, Robert. *A Concise History of South Africa.* Cambridge Universi-ty Press, 1999.

Ruane, Michael E. "China was a brutal communist menace. In 1972, Richard Nixon visited, anyway." *Washington Post*, Feb. 20, 2022. https://www.washingtonpost.com/history/2022/02/20/nixon-china-mao-visit-1972.

Sanchez, Jesse. "MLB wraps 'exhilarating' goodwill trip to Cuba." MLB. Last modified Dec. 17, 2015. https://www.mlb.com/news/mlb-finishes-positive-goodwill-tour-of-cuba/c-159948056#.

Sanders, Barry. "Sport as Public Diplomacy." *Sports Diplomacy* 2, no. 6 (2011). https://uscpublicdiplomacy.org/pdin_monitor_article/sport-public-diplomacy.

Sands, Lee M. "The 2008 Olympics' Impact on China." *China Business Review*, July 1, 2008. https://www.chinabusinessreview.com/the-2008-olympics-impact-on-china.

Sargsyan, Serzh. "We Are Ready to Talk to Turkey." *Wall Street Journal*, July 9, 2008. https://wsj.com/articles/SB121555668872637291.

Scurr, Cory. "Cold War by 'Other Means': Canada's Foreign Relations with Communist Eastern Europe, 1957-1963." *Theses and Dissertations (Comprehensive)*, 1989. Wilfrid Laurier University Press, 2017.

Sebastian, Meryl and Sharanya Hrishikesh. "Article 370: India Supreme Court upholds repeal of Kashmir's special status." BBC News. Last modified Dec. 11, 2023. https://www.bbc.com/news/world-asia-india-67634689

Sin, Ben. "NBA Looks to Asia for Next Growth Spurt." *New York Times*, March 14, 2014. http://www.nytimes.com/2014/03/15/business/international/nba-looks-to-asia-for-next-growth-spurt.html.

Sinden, Harry. *Hockey Showdown: The Canada-Russia Hockey Series*. Doubleday Canada, 1972.

Skidelsky, Robert. "Can the Olympics Prevent War?" Project Syndicate. Last modified Feb. 15, 2022. https://www.project-syndicate.org/commentary/olympic-dream-sport-politics-and-ukraine-by-robert-skidelsky-2022-02.

Snelling, Dennis. "The Greatest Piece of Diplomacy Ever: The 1949 Tour of Lefty O'Doul and the San Francisco Seals." In Nichibei Yakyu, *US Tours of Japan, 1907-1958*. Society for American Baseball Research, 2022.

Sprter. "From the Pitch to Power: Three Athletes Who Made the Transition from Sport to Politics." Last modified April 5, 2018. https://sprter.com/uncategorized/athletes-in-politics.

Staples, Bill, Jr. *Kenichi Zenimura, Japanese American Baseball Pioneer*. McFarland & Company, 2011.

"Story Behind Book Donation." *Gila News Courier*, Dec. 31, 1943. https://ddr.densho.org/ddr-densho-141-211.

Strenk, Andrew. "Diplomats in Track Suits: the Role of Sports in the Foreign Policy of the German Democratic Republic." *Journal of Sport and Social Issues* 4, no 1 (1980): 34-45.

Su, Jingjing and Daqing Zhang. "A study on the first medical delegation from New China to the United States." Science Spring. Last modified Aug.14, 2017. https://baike.baidu.com/tashuo/browse/content?id=b05f0ad88174b62e06440318.

Suzuki, Bunshiro. "U.S.-Japanese Baseball and Japanese Spectators." *Yomiuri Shimbun*, Oct. 29, 1949.

Sweig, Julia E. *Cuba: What Everyone Needs to Know*. Oxford University Press, 2016.

Szymanski, Stefan. "Why Maradona's 'Hand of God' goal is priceless – and unforgettable." *The Conversation*, Nov. 19, 2022. https://theconversation.com/why-maradonas-hand-of-god-goal-is-priceless-and-unforgettable-193760.

Taylor, David. "Iran vs USA and the most political moments in World Cup history." *GQ Magazine*, Nov. 29, 2022. https://www.gq-magazine.co.uk/sport/gallery/most-political-moments-in-world-cup-history.

The Paper. "The Shanghai Communiqué and their lives: 50 years of Sino-US people-to-people exchanges." Last modified Feb. 28, 2022. https://mil.sina.cn/zgjq/2022-02-28/detail-imcwipih5869452.d.html.

Thomas, Clem. 1995. "We had 43 million behind us." *Independent*,

June 24, 1995. https://www.independent.co.uk/sport/we-had-43-million-behind-us-1588137.html.

Time, 1971. "The World: The Ping Heard Round the World." Last modified Apr. 26, 1971.

"To Overcome Prejudice Barriers." *Gila News Courier*, Mar. 9, 1943. https://ddr.densho.org/ddr-densho-141-65.

Trotta, Daniel and Sarah Marsh. "Cuban deal with MLB allows players to sign without defecting." Reuters. Last modified Dec. 19, 2018. https://www.reuters.com/article/sports/cuban-deal-with-mlb-allows-players-to-sign-without-defecting-idUSKCN1OI2L5.

Trusdell, Brian. *Miracle on Ice*. ABDO Publishing Company, 2015.

Tucker, Nancy Bernkopf. "China as a Factor in the Collapse of the Soviet Empire." *Political Science Quarterly* 110, no. 4 (1995): 501–18.

"Two Evacuees Work for Carl Sandberg in Michigan." *Gila News Courier*, Mar. 9, 1944. https://ddr.densho.org/ddr-densho-141-241.

United Nations. "Geneva Agreements 20-21 July 1954." Entered into force July 20, 1954. https://peacemaker.un.org/sites/default/files/document/files/2024/05/kh-la-vn540720gene-vaagreements.pdf.

United Nations. "International Convention on the Suppression and Punishment of the Crime of Apartheid." Entered into force July 18, 1976. https://www.un.org/en/genocideprevention/documents/atrocity-crimes/Doc.10_International%20Convention%20on%20the%20Suppression%20and%20Punishment%20of%20the%20Crime%20of%20Apartheid.pdf.

United Nations. "The United Nations and the Olympic Truce." Accessed July 23, 2024. https://www.un.org/en/olympictruce.

UPI. "Foreign Policy: Red China and Russia." Last modified 1971. https://www.upi.com/Archives/Audio/Events-of-1971/Foreign-Policy-Red-China-and-Russia.

US Department of State. "US Interests Section." Accessed July 7, 2024. https://1997-2001.state.gov/regions/wha/cuba/usint.

html.

Valenzuela, Janine Romero. "Integration through sports." Accessed July 7, 2024. https://globalcompactrefugees.org/good-practices/integration-through-sports.

VICE. "North Korea and Harlem Globetrotters' Diplomacy Basketball Lunch (VICE on HBO)." Last modified June 14, 2013. https://www.youtube.com/watch?v=BoeSlDeb3NY.

Waleik, Gary. "When North Joined South: The Story Of The Unified Korean Olympic Ice Hockey Team." *Wbur.* Last modified Jan. 10, 2020. https://www.wbur.org/onlygame/2020/01/10/south-korea-north-korea-unified-hockey-pyeongchang-olympics-book.

Walker, Nigel. "Conflict in Ukraine: A timeline (current conflict, 2022 – present)." UK Parliament House of Commons Library. Accessed June 16, 2024. https://commonslibrary.parliament.uk/research-briefings/cbp-9847.

Walshe, Peter. *The Rise of Nationalism in South Afraid: The African National Congress, 1912-195.* Hurst, 1970.

Wang, Guanhua. "'Friendship First': China's Sports Diplomacy during the Cold War." *The Journal of American-East Asian Relations* 12, no. 3/4 (2003): 133–53.

Watkins, Calvin. "Rockets celebrate Yao Ming as Hall of Famer's No. 11 jersey retired." ESPN, Last modified Feb. 3, 2017. https://www.espn.com/nba/story/_/id/18615456/houston-rockets-retire-yao-ming-no11-jersey-friday-night.

Weintraub, Stanley. *Silent Night: The Story of the World War I Christmas Truce.* Plume, 2001.

Wilmot, Joe. "It All Adds Up to 'O'Douro, We Love You.'" *San Francisco Chronicle*, Feb. 6, 1950.

Wilson, J. J. "27 remarkable days: the 1972 summit series of ice hockey between Canada and the Soviet Union." *Totalitarian Movements and Political Religions* 5, no 2 (2004): 271–280.

Wisensale, Steven. "How Baseball Has Strengthened the Relationship Between the United States and Japan." *Smithsonian*

Magazine, Mar. 29, 2018. https://www.smithsonianmag.com/history/how-baseball-strengthened-relationship-between-united-states-japan-180968597.

Xinhua News Agency. "Cultural Exchange Bridges China and US." Last modified Feb. 15, 2002. http://www.china.org.cn/english/2002/Feb/27044.htm.

Yomiuri Shimbun. "O'Doul Expresses Thanks to Japanese Fans." *Yomiuri Shimbun*, Oct. 28, 1949.

Zhang, Jing. "The Origins, Practices, and Narratives of Sino-American Civilian Technological Exchanges (1971-1978)." *The Chinese Journal of American Studies* 5: 122-160. www.hist.pku.edu.cn/docs/2021-09/90234545bb6a46d8a5dc647bc9b-9f3cc.pdf.

Zhao, Qizheng. "From People-to-People Diplomacy to Public Diplomacy, Reflecting a Sense of Responsibility and Patriotism." *People's Daily Overseas Edition*, Oct. 9, 2009. http://www.cppcc.gov.cn/2011/09/07/ARTI1315357310343515.shtml.

Zhou, Liangjun, Jerred Junqi Wang, Xiaoying Chen, Chundong Lei, James J. Zhang and Xiao Meng. "The development of NBA in China: a glocalization perspective." *International Journal of Sports Marketing and Sponsorship* 18. no. 1 (2017): 81-94.

Zhou, May. "NBA does a slam-dunk in China," *China Daily*, April 4, 2014. http://usa.chinadaily.com.cn/epaper/2014-04/04/content_17409032.htm.

ABOUT THE AUTHOR

Yifei Kevin Niu is the founder and editor-in-chief of *The GOAT*, a sports newspaper. When he's not playing or writing about sports, Kevin enjoys traveling, history, poetry, and creative nonfiction. He is passionate about educating youth worldwide about people-to-people diplomacy and encouraging underprivileged students to gain confidence in their writing, using sports as a platform. Kevin lives with his parents and sister in New York. This is his first book.

ABOUT THE PUBLISHER

Di Angelo Publications was founded in 2008 by Sequoia Schmidt to provide an inclusive platform for sharing impactful experiences and powerful stories. The modernized publishing firm's creative headquarters is in Los Angeles, California. The firm publishes 14 new titles a year across 10 imprints spanning multiple genres, representing Grammy Award winners, a congresswoman, multiple actors, and NYT bestsellers. The featured imprint, Erudition, was inspired by the desire to spread knowledge, spark curiosity, and add numbers to the ranks of continuing learners, big and small.